CPC PRACTICE EXAM

Certified Professional Coder:
2015 – 2016 Practice Test Questions

FREE *FROM STRESS TO SUCCESS* DVD FROM TRIVIUM TEST PREP

Dear Customer,

Thank you for purchasing from Trivium Test Prep! Whether you're looking to join the military, get into college, or advance your career, we're honored to be a part of your journey.

To show our appreciation (and to help you relieve a little of that test-prep stress), we're offering a **FREE *From Stress to Success* DVD** by Trivium Test Prep. Our DVD includes 35 test preparation strategies that will help keep you calm and collected before and during your big exam. All we ask is that you email us your feedback and describe your experience with our product. Amazing, awful, or just so-so: we want to hear what you have to say!

To receive your **FREE *From Stress to Success* DVD**, please email us at 5star@triviumtestprep. com. Include "Free 5 Star" in the subject line and the following information in your email:

1. The title of the product you purchased.

2. Your rating from 1 – 5 (with 5 being the best).

3. Your feedback about the product, including how our materials helped you meet your goals and ways in which we can improve our products.

4. Your full name and shipping address so we can send your **FREE *From Stress to Success* DVD**.

If you have any questions or concerns please feel free to contact me directly.

Thank you, and good luck with your studies!

Alyssa Wagoner
Quality Control
alyssa.wagoner@triviumtestprep.com

TABLE OF CONTENTS

INTRODUCTION   i

TEST YOUR KNOWLEDGE   1

TEST YOUR KNOWLEDGE – ANSWERS   26

INTRODUCTION

The American Academy of Professional Coders (AAPC) offers the Certified Professional Coder (CPC®), which is the highest standard for medical coding in physician office settings. CPC® is vital for a compliant and lucrative medical practice, but it also increases a coder's chances of being hired, and significantly increases a coder's salary.

This study guide provides everything a coder needs to know in order to pass the CPC examination and receive the credential. By way of this examination, the coder will prove that he or she knows how to read a medical chart and assign the correct diagnosis (ICD-9 or ICD-10), procedure (CPT®), and supply (HCPCS Level II) codes for numerous clinical situations and services.

Founded in 1988, the AAPC offers professional certification to physician-based medical coders and also provide networking and educational opportunities. At present, AAPC has over 125,000 members worldwide, and as many as 100,000 of them are certified coders. Credentialed coders who hold the CPC title have proven mastery of code sets, as well as knowledge of management standards, evaluation principles, and documentation guidelines.

CPC® abilities include the following:

- The CPC has expertise in medical coding rules and regulations, including reimbursement and compliance, which allows the coder to handle issues effectively, such as claim denials and bundling problems.
- The CPC is proficient in reviewing and assigning accurate medical codes for diagnoses, procedures and healthcare services performed by a variety of healthcare providers.
- The CPC has a sound knowledge of evaluation and management services, anesthesia and surgical services, as well as radiology, pathology, and medical services.
- The CPC has the ability to successfully manage the integration of rule changes and medical coding alterations into a practice's reimbursement processes.

THE CPC® EXAM

The CPC® exam includes 150 multiple-choice questions in which five hours and forty minutes is allotted for completion. The exam costs $260 for AAPC students, and $325 for everyone else, which includes one free retake. During the exam, a code book is provided.

The CPC® exam consists of questions regarding the correct application of CPT®, HCPCS Level II procedure and supply codes, and ICD-9-CM and ICD-10-CM diagnosis codes. The purpose of the test is to evaluate a physician practice coder's competence and knowledge of the following:

- anesthesia
- radiology
- medicine
- nervous system
- endocrine system
- digestive system
- musculoskeletal system
- evaluation and management
- anatomy and physiology
- mediastinum and diaphragm
- practice management
- male and female genitalia

- hemic and lymphatic system
- maternity and delivery
- eye and ocular adnexa
- ICD-9-CM
- HCPCS Level II
- coding guidelines
- medical terminology
- pathology
- integumentary
- respiratory
- laboratory

CONCLUSION

Here at Trivium Test Prep our hope is that we not only taught you the relevant information needed to pass the exam, but that we helped you exceed all previous expectations. Our goal is to keep our guides concise, show you a few test tricks along the way, and ultimately help you succeed in your goals.

On that note, we are always interested in your feedback. To let us know if we've truly prepared you for the exam, please email us at feedback@triviumtestprep.com. Feel free to include your test score!

Your success is our success. Good luck on the exam and your future ventures.

Sincerely,

-*Trivium Test Prep Team*-

TEST YOUR KNOWLEDGE

1. **The integument (skin) makes up what percent of the body's overall weight?**

   A. 5%

   B. 12%

   C. 18%

   D. 22%

2. **What is the function of the skin?**

   A. regulate body temperature

   B. manufacture vitamins

   C. protect from microorganisms

   D. all of the above

3. **The outermost layer of skin is:**

   A. epidermis

   B. dermis

   C. hypodermis

   D. subcutaneous

4. **The sebaceous glands are in the:**

   A. epidermis

   B. dermis

   C. hypodermis

   D. subcutaneous

5. **Anhidrosis is:**

   A. too much or increased sweat

   B. lack of or decreased sweat

   C. too much or increased oil

   D. lack of or decreased oil

6. **Which of the following is a fatty tissue tumor?**

   A. adipose

   B. hematoma

   C. lipoma

   D. steatoma

7. **Which type of dermatitis is common in young children?**

   A. atopic

   B. contact

   C. stasis

   D. seborrheic

8. **An irregular shaped, elevated scar that occurs from excessive collagen in the corneum during tissue repair is:**

   A. macule

   B. papule

   C. keloid

   D. nodule

9. **A fissure is:**

   A. skin cracks, such as athlete's foot, or cracks in the corners of the mouth

   B. loss of a portion of the skin, which is a physiologic response to aging

   C. temporary, localized skin elevation, such as an insect bite or allergic reaction

   D. dried skin exudate (scab)

10. **Which of the following skin conditions is associated with a herald patch?**

    A. stasis dermatitis

    B. psoriasis

    C. pityriasis rosea

    D. none of the above

11. **Which skin tumor is benign?**

    A. melanoma

    B. kaposi's sarcoma

    C. keratoacanthoma

    D. · basal cell carcinoma

12. **Which infection that results from injury and is caused by Staphylococcus?**

    A. cellulitis

    B. folliculitis

    C. furuncle

    D. impetigo

13. **This infection is caused by the herpes virus:**

    A. cold sores of the mouth

    B. genital sores

    C. shingles

    D. all of the above

14. **Which form of tinea occurs on the feet?**

    A. manis

    B. capitus

    C. corporis

    D. pedis

15. **Which of the following is NOT a symptom of acne vulgaris?**

    A. blackheads

    B. pustules

    C. macules

    D. papules

16. **How many bones are in the human body?**

    A. 100

    B. 106

    C. 200

    D. 206

17. **Which of the following is NOT considered to be a long bone?**

    A. femur

    B. scapula

    C. tibia

    D. humerus

18. **Which of the following is NOT one of the middle ear bones?**

    A. malleus

    B. ethmoid

    C. incus

    D. stapes

19. **Which facial bone is the cheekbone?**

    A. maxilla

    B. nasal

    C. zygomatic

    D. vomer

20. **What is the upper portion of the pelvis called?**

    A. pubis symphysis

    B. ischium

    C. pubis

    D. ilium

21. **This bone is the smaller of the two lower arm bones:**

   A. radius

   B. ulna

   C. humerus

   D. talus

22. **Which type of tissue lines the bowel, blood vessels, and urethra?**

   A. visceral

   B. skeletal

   C. cardiac

   D. none of the above

23. **Which of the following muscles is not matched with the appropriate action?**

   A. trapezius – extends head

   B. deltoid – abducts upper arm

   C. sternocleidomastoid – grates teeth

   D. pectoralis major – flexes upper arm

24. **Which of the following pertains to cartilage?**

   A. chondral

   B. ganglion

   C. articular

   D. bursa

25. **This injury is a compound break where the bone penetrates the skin:**

   A. complete fracture

   B. incomplete fracture

   C. open fracture

   D. closed fracture

26. **What causes osteomyelitis?**

   A. advancing age

   B. bacteria

   C. viruses

   D. decreased bone mass

27. **This joint disorder is caused by excessive uric acid:**

   A. spina bifida

   B. septic arthritis

   C. gouty arthritis

   D. ankylosing spondylosis

28. **Which condition has a genetic predisposition?**

   A. polymyositis

   B. fibromylagia

   C. muscular dystrophy

   D. all of the above

29. **Which bone tumor is usually benign?**

   A. chondroblastoma

   B. multiple myeloma

   C. rhabdomyosarcoma

   D. osteosarcoma

30. **Which type of arthritis is considered to be an autoimmune disease?**

   A. osteoarthritis

   B. rheumatoid arthritis

   C. septic arthritis

   D. gouty arthritis

31. **Which of the following is NOT part of the lower respiratory tract?**

   A. turbinates

   B. bronchial tree

   C. trachea

   D. lungs

32. **Which structure is considered the voicebox?**

   A. pharynx

   B. larynx

   C. turbinates

   D. conchae

33. **When the skin or lips are bluish, this is called:**

   A. asphyxia

   B. cyanosis

   C. orthopnea

   D. tachypnea

34. **The physician has documented nose bleed in the medical record. To code this visit, what would you search for in the Alphabetic Index?**

   A. atelectasis

   B. epitaxis

   C. cyanosis

   D. pleuritis

35. **The patient has documented symptoms of hemoptysis and rhinorrhea and no existing diagnosis. What do these terms mean?**

   A. The patient is coughing up blood and has drainage from the nose.

   B. The patient is coughing up sputum and has blood draining from the nose.

   C. The patient has lung and nose pain.

   D. none of the above

36. **What condition is acute injury to the alveolocapillary membrane, which results in atelectasis and edema?**

   A. acute respiratory failure

   B. respiratory acidosis

   C. pneumothorax

   D. adult respiratory distress syndrome (ARDS)

37. **The chronic dilation of the bronchi associated with bronchiectasis can be:**

   A. cylindrical

   B. varicose

   C. cystic

   D. all of the above

38. **Which of the following is not a substance that lodges in a pulmonary artery and causes a pulmonary embolism?**

   A. air

   B. blood clot

   C. tissue

   D. pus

39. **With an empyema, there is pus in:**

   A. the pleural space

   B. the pulmonary artery

   C. the bronchioles

   D. the lung tissue

40. **Which of the following is NOT a form of Chronic Obstructive Pulmonary Disease (COPD)?**

   A. chronic bronchitis

   B. emphysema

   C. pneumonia

   D. All of the above are forms of COPD.

41. **When there is increased carbon dioxide in the arterial blood caused by poor alveoli ventilation, the condition is called:**

   A. hypoxemia

   B. hypercapnia

   C. bronchiectasis

   D. bronchiolitis

42. **With respiratory acidosis, what happens to the pH level?**

   A. It goes up.

   B. It goes down.

   C. It stays the same.

   D. It fluctuates.

43. **With pneumoconiosis, particles invade the lung tissue, such as:**

   A. blood clots, air, or cholesterol

   B. pus, fluid, and White Blood Cells (WBCs)

   C. coal, asbestos, or fiberglass

   D. all of the above

44. **What lung condition is often caused by an upper respiratory infection?**

    A. pneumoconiosis

    B. pulmonary embolism (PE)

    C. pleurisy

    D. COPD

45. **What is the function of the respiratory tract?**

    A. supply the body with oxygen

    B. rid the body of carbon dioxide

    C. both A. and B.

    D. neither A. nor B.

46. **What component of the cardiovascular system transports nutrients and hormones?**

    A. the heart

    B. the blood

    C. the vessels

    D. all of the above

47. **What percentage of water is plasma?**

    A. 9%

    B. 19%

    C. 91%

    D. 99%

48. **All of the following are part of cellular blood EXCEPT:**

    A. plasma

    B. leukocytes

    C. thrombocytes

    D. erythrocytes

49. **The vessels that lead away from the heart are the:**

    A. veins

    B. arteries

    C. capillaries

    D. venules

50. **How many heart chambers are there?**

    A. two

    B. three

    C. four

    D. six

51. **Which valve lies between the right atrium and the right ventricle?**

    A. aortic

    B. pulmonary

    C. tricuspid

    D. bicuspid

52. **A physician has documented that a blood clot lies in the *epicardial* region. What does this mean?**

    A. under the heart

    B. over the heart

    C. beside the heart

    D. around the heart

53. **With the hemolysis process, what substance is broken down?**

    A. WBCs

    B. leukocytes

    C. RBCs

    D. plaque

54. **The physician has performed an atherectomy. What was removed?**

    A. embolism

    B. blood vessel

    C. pus

    D. plaque

55. **Which of the following is NOT a risk factor for Coronary Artery Disease (CAD)?**

    A. advanced age

    B. smoking

    C. diabetes

    D. trauma

56. **Which of the following is another name for a heart attack?**

    A. ischemic heart disease

    B. Myocardial Infarction (MI)

    C hypertension

    D. aneurysm

57. **All of the following can cause a thrombus EXCEPT:**

    A. infection

    B. inflammation

    C. atherosclerosis

    D. ischemia

58. **Symptoms of hypotension include:**

    A. dizziness, blurred vision, and syncope

    B. nosebleeds and cough

    C. crushing chest pain and irritability

    D. none of the above

59. **Another name for Peripheral Artery Disease (PAD) is:**

    A. Burger's disease

    B. Buerger's disease

    C. Bogoer's disease

    D. Biguer's disease

60. **A group of cardiac diseases that affect the myocardium are:**

    A. arrhythmias

    B. rheumatic heart diseases

    C. cardiomyopathies

    D. valvular diseases

61. **What type of cells has been known to cause an embolism?**

    A. cancer cells

    B. skin cells

    C. brain cells

    D. nerve cells

62. **A patient with varicosities will have what symptoms?**

    A. leg pain and swelling

    B. leg redness and warmth

    C. leg vasospasms

    D. leg cyanosis

63. **Which of the following is NOT a cause of infective endocarditis?**

    A. bacteria

    B. viruses

    C. fungi

    D. blood clots

64. **Which arrhythmia results in rapid, erratic contractions of the heart?**

    A. ventricular fibrillation

    B. atrial fibrillation (A. fib)

    C. atrial flutter

    D. asystole

65. **How many types of pericarditis are there?**

    A. one

    B. two

    C. three

    D. four

66. **What is the function of the female reproductive external structures?**

    A. enhance sexual stimulation

    B. protect the body from foreign material

    C. both A and B

    D. neither A nor B

67. **Which uterine layer is the middle one?**

    A. endometrium

    B. myometrium

    C. perimetrium

    D. vulva

68. **The phase of mensuration that spans from day six through day twelve is the:**

    A. proliferation phase

    B. endometrium repair

    C. secretory phase

    D. premenstruation

69. **How many days is human gestation?**

    A. 166

    B. 236

    C. 266

    D. 336

70. **The third trimester starts at what week of the pregnancy?**

    A. last menstrual period (LMP)

    B. thirteen

    C. twenty-eight

    D. thirty-three

71. **The physician has discovered a pregnancy that is *ectopic*. What does this mean?**

    A. occurred inside the uterus

    B. occurred outside the uterus

    C. termination of pregnancy

    D. more than one pregnancy

72. **A physician documents that there is a lesion at the area between the vagina and anus. What term does this imply?**

    A. cystocele

    B. antepartum

    C. introitus

    D. perineum

73. **A woman is experiencing pelvic cramping at the start of menstruation. What is the medical term to use?**

    A. primary dysmenorrhea

    B. secondary dysmenorrhea

    C. primary menorrhagia

    D. secondary menorrhagia

74. **For a condition to be considered primary amenorrhea, which of the following must be true?**

    A. Menstruation ceases for three cycles.

    B. Menstruation ceases for six cycles.

    C. Menstruation ceases for one year.

    D. Menstruation has never occurred.

75. **All of the following can cause secondary menstruation EXCEPT:**

    A. stress

    B. certain foods

    C. eating disorders

    D. strenuous exercise

76. **Irregular menstrual cycles of varying duration and amounts is called:**

    A. metorrhagia

    B. menorrhagia

    C. hypomenorrhea

    D. menometorrhagia

77. **Which vaginal infection causes white, curd-like vaginal discharge?**

    A. pelvic inflammatory disease

    B. gonorrhea

    C. chlamydia

    D. candidiasis

78. **Which of the following is caused by the human papillomavirus?**

    A. pelvic inflammatory disease

    B. herpes

    C. condylomata

    D. gonorrhea

79. **Which condition of pregnancy is characterized by edema, hypertension, and proteinuria?**

    A. amenorrhea

    B. placental previa

    C. eclampsia

    D. adenomyosis

80. **A vaginal infection caused by a protozoan is:**

A. candidiasis

B. trichomoniasis

C. chlamydia

D. gonorrhea

81. **When a lesion occurs beneath the endometrium, what is the correct term to describe that lesion?**

A. intramural

B. subserosa

C. submucous

D. intermucus

82. **What structure of the male reproduction system produces sperm?**

A. prostate gland

B. seminal vesicles

C. bulbourethral gland

D. testes

83. **The structure that lies at the end of the epididymis is:**

A. prostate gland

B. seminal ducts

C. vas deferens

D. testes

84. **What is the surgical procedure to lower undescended testis?**

A. orchiopexy

B. prostatotomy

C. vasectomy

D. transurethral resection of the prostate (TURP)

85. **Which condition can cause severe pain, nausea, vomiting, edema, and fever?**

A. cryptorchidism

B. orchitis

C. prostatitis

D. testicular torsion

86. **Epididymitis is caused from all of the following EXCEPT:**

A. scrotal pain

B. trauma

C. injury

D. infection

87. **The two cavities inside the penis are known as the:**

A. epididymis

B. chordee

C. corpora cavernosa

D. varicocele

88. **The physician documents that the urethral meatus is mislocated to the dorsal side of penis. What is this called?**

A. testicular torsion

B. erispadias

C. hypospadias

D. phimosis

89. **What male reproductive system infection often is caused by E. coli bacteria and causes suprapubic pain, dysuria, and fever?**

A. orchitis

B. prostatitis

C. benign prostatic hypertrophy

D. paraphimosis

90. **What condition is caused by increased levels of hormones and fibrous nodules?**

A. phimosis

B. urethritis

C. prostatitis

D. benign prostatic hyperplasia (BPH)

91. **What congenital condition of the penis results in the foreskin constricted and retracted over the penis?**

A. phimosis

B. paraphimosis

C. BPH

D. chordee

92. **Which of the following is NOT a component of the urinary system?**

   A. bladder

   B. ureters

   C. urethra

   D. pancreas

93. **What is the outer portion of the kidney called?**

   A. papilla

   B. hilum

   C. medullar

   D. cortex

94. **Which procedure involves surgical repair of the urethra?**

   A. cystoplasty

   B. cystoscopy

   C. ureterotomy

   D. urethroplasty

95. **All of the following is a type of acute renal failure EXCEPT:**

   A. interrenal

   B. intrarenal

   C. prerenal

   D. postrenal

96. **Which of the following is NOT a symptom of acute pyelonephritis?**

   A. dysuria

   B. hypertension

   C. fever

   D. nocturia

97. **What kidney infection is caused by Streptococcus?**

   A. cystitis

   B. acute pyelonephritis

   C. acute poststerptococcal glomerulonephritis (APSAGN)

   D. nephrolithiasis

98. **Of the following kidney conditions, which one is genetic?**

   A. APSAGN

   B. BPH

   C. COPD

   D. polycystic kidney disease (PKD)

99. **Which of the following regulates the gastrointestinal (GI) tract?**

   A. local control system

   B. hormonal system

   C. neural system

   D. all of the above

100. **How many permanent teeth do adults have?**

   A. 22

   B. 30

   C. 32

   D. 36

101. **Which organ stores bile?**

   A. liver

   B. gallbladder

   C. pancreas

   D. stomach

102. **What procedure examines the sigmoid colon and rectum via a small scope?**

   A. cholecystectomy

   B. colonoscopy

   C. laparoscopy

   D. proctosigmoidoscopy

103. **What is a hernia?**

   A. tissue or organ protruding through a cavity or the abdominal wall

   B. protrusion in the wall of the colon

   C. varicose veins

   D. artificial opening between the stomach and the abdominal wall

104. **A canker sore is also called a:**

    A. aphthous ulcer

    B. aphthous stomatitis

    C. aphthous ulceration

    D. all of the above

105. **What infantile condition causes failure to thrive and projectile vomiting?**

    A. scleroderma

    B. pyloric stenosis

    C. hiatal hernia

    D. gastritis

106. **Which inflammatory condition causes diarrhea, gas, and abdominal pain, and is associated with aging?**

    A. cirrhosis

    B. appendicitis

    C. diverticulitis

    D. pancreatitis

107. **A small structure of concentrated lymph tissue is called:**

    A. thymus

    B. tonsil

    C. lymph node

    D. spleen

108. **Which lymph nodes are located in the armpits?**

    A. axillary nodes

    B. jugular nodes

    C. submental nodes

    D. inguinal nodes

109. **Which type of anemia is caused by blood loss, low iron intake, and poor iron absorption?**

    A. aplastic anemia

    B. iron deficiency anemia

    C. sickle cell anemia

    D. hemolytic anemia

110. **Which disease involves cancer of the blood that occurs more often in children and adolescents and is caused by immature lymphocytes?**

    A. chronic myelogenous leukemia (CML)

    B. chronic lymphocytic leukemia (CLL)

    C. acute myelogenous leukemia (AML)

    D. acute lymphocytic leukemia (ALL)

111. **The function of the endocrine system is to:**

    A. produce RBCs

    B. regulate thermogenesis

    C. provide structural support

    D. manage various body functions by use of hormones

112. **Which gland is located at the base of the brain near the sella turica?**

    A. thyroid gland

    B. parathyroid gland

    C. pituitary gland

    D. adrenal gland

113. **Which hormone-releasing gland is located above the pituitary gland?**

    A. thymus

    B. pancreas

    C. hypothalamus

    D. pineal gland

114. **Which type of diabetes mellitus causes polyuria, polydipsia, and glycosuria?**

    A. type I

    B. type II

    C. both A and B

    D. neither A nor B

115. **What causes Cushing's syndrome?**

    A. an autoimmune process

    B. inadequate amounts of thyroid stimulating hormone (TSH) or poor thyroid

    C. tumors, viruses, autoimmune disorders, infection, and tuberculosis

    D. an overactive adrenal cortex or long-term use of steroids

116. **What are two components of the peripheral nervous system (PNS)?**

    A. the cranial nerves and the spinal nerves

    B. the brain and the spinal cord

    C. the axon and the myelin sheath

    D. the cerebellum and the cerebrum

117. **How many lumbar vertebrae are there?**

    A. 4

    B. 5

    C. 7

    D. 12

118. **Surgical removal of a disc is called:**

    A. craniectomy

    B. laminectomy

    C. vertebrectomy

    D. discectomy

119. **What reversible condition produces slurred speech, paresthesia of face, and mental confusion?**

    A. Alzheimer's disease

    B. transient ischemic attack (TIA)

    C. amyotrophic lateral sclerosis

    D. myasthenia gravis (MG)

120. **Which sense is associated with cranial nerve one (CN1)?**

    A. touch

    B. sight

    C. smell

    D. hearing

121. **Fluid in front of the lens is called:**

    A. sclera

    B. vitreous humor

    C. aqueous humor

    D. choroid

122. **Which of the following is also called the eardrum?**

    A. ossicle

    B. stapes

    C. auricle

    D. tympanic membrane

123. **What is ptosis?**

    A. drooping of the upper eyelid

    B. blocked nasolacrimal duct

    C. eyelid inflammation

    D. nearsightedness

124. **A physician documents that he created a small opening in the middle ear. What is this called?**

    A. apicectomy

    B. mastoidectomy

    C. keratoplasty

    D. fenestration

125. **Macular degeneration is:**

    A. destruction of the fovea centralis

    B. age-related

    C. loss of central vision

    D. all of the above

126. **Which type of hearing loss is caused by a lesion of the cochlea or neural path that results in a defect in receptors or the vestibulocochlear nerve?**

    A. conductive hearing loss

    B. sensorineural hearing loss

    C. both A and B

    D. neither A nor B

127. **A hordelolum is also called:**

    A. pink eye

    B. a stye

    C. clouding of the lens

    D. corneal inflammation

128. **What is volume 1 of the *International Classification of Diseases* (ICD) Ninth Revision (9) Clinical Modifications (CM) manual (ICD-9-CM) called?**

    A. Diseases, Tabular

    B. Diseases, Index

    C. Hospital Version

    D. none of the above

129. **Which ICD-9 convention is used to enclose synonyms, explanatory phrases, and alternative wording?**

    A. brackets

    B. parentheses

    C. colons

    D. braces

130. **What ICD-9 codes are used to provide additional information regarding the exact nature of injury or poisoning?**

    A. V codes

    B. E codes

    C. Z codes

    D. none of the above

131. **What is the purpose of an inclusion note?**

    A. to indicate that the terms excluded from the code should be used somewhere else

    B. to specify the conditions for which that code number is to be used

    C. to further define or give examples of the content

    D. all of the above

132. **Which of the following is NOT one of the organizations who developed the ICD-9-CM coding guidelines?**

    A. American Health Information Management Association (AHIMA)

    B. American Hospital Association (AHA)

    C. Centers for Medicare and Medicaid Services (CMS)

    D. American Medical Association (AMA)

133. **Codes that describe the signs and symptoms rather than a diagnosis are only first-listed when:**

    A. An existing diagnosis is on the patient's problem list.

    B. An existing diagnosis is in the nurses notes.

    C. No diagnosis is established or confirmed by a physician.

    D. They best describe the illness.

134. **Chronic condition codes can be used:**

    A. as long as the patient is receiving care for that diagnosis

    B. only once

    C. only when there is an exacerbation of the chronic illness

    D. never

135. **If routine testing is performed during the same encounter to evaluate a sign, symptom, or diagnosis, the coder should:**

    A. Assign first a code describing the reason for the non-routine test, followed by a secondary V code.

    B. Assign the V code first, followed by a secondary code describing the reason for the non-routine test.

    C. Assign a combination code.

    D. none of the above

136. **For a patient who is receiving chemotherapy, radiation therapy, or rehabilitation, the coder should:**

A. Use an appropriate diagnosis code first, followed by a secondary code for the treatment.

B. Use a combination code for the therapy and the diagnosis.

C. Use an appropriate V code first, followed by a secondary code for the diagnosis or problem that requires treatment.

D. Use an appropriate E code first, followed by a secondary code for the diagnosis or problem that requires treatment.

137. **When an episode of healthcare involves a number of related conditions, and when no one condition predominates, the coder should:**

A. Use a code that represents the most demanding medical condition.

B. Use a code that incorporates multiple conditions as the *main* code.

C. Use a code that represents the worst medical condition, followed by secondary codes for all other diagnoses.

D. none of the above

138. **A thirty-six-year-old man has returned for his human immunodeficiency virus (HIV) test results, and he was recently found to be HIV positive. What should the coder use for this encounter?**

A. 795.71 Nonspecific HIV serology

B. 042 HIV

C. V73.89 Screening for other specified viral disease

D. V65.44 HIV counseling

139. **When coding for a neoplasm, what should the coder do first?**

A. Go to the Neoplasm Table in the Alphabetic Index.

B. Locate the histologic type.

C. Find the code by body site.

D. Locate the neoplasm in the Tabular List.

140. **When therapy is given to a patient with cancer, the coder should:**

A. First code for the treatment, followed by a secondary neoplasm code.

B. First code for the neoplasm, followed by a secondary code for the treatment.

C. Use a combination code for the neoplasm and the treatment.

D. Use a Z code for the medication, followed by secondary codes for treatment and diagnosis.

141. **A patient with bone cancer is having a reduction procedure for a broken radius (right arm). What should be coded first?**

A. the neoplasm

B. the fracture

C. a code for the procedure

D. none of the above

142. **For a patient with extensive metastasis where the physician is unable to determine the site of primary malignancy, what code should be used?**

A. disseminated malignant neoplasm, unspecified

B. multiple neoplasms, not otherwise specified

C. malignant neoplasm, unspecified

D. any of the above

143. **When it is documented that the patient uses insulin, but the type of diabetes is not recorded, the coder should use:**

A. a code for Long-term use of insulin, followed by a secondary code for Type I diabetes mellitus

B. a code for Long-term use of insulin, followed by a secondary code for Type II diabetes mellitus

C. a code for Type I diabetes mellitus, followed by a secondary code for Long-term use of insulin

D. a code for Type II diabetes mellitus, followed by a secondary code for Long-term use of insulin

144. **If the type of diabetes mellitus is not documented in the medical record, the default diagnosis is:**

A. type I diabetes

B. type II diabetes

C. juvenile diabetes

D. diabetes

145. **For an encounter due to an insulin pump malfunction resulting in an overdose of insulin, the coder should:**

A. Assign code 996.57, Mechanical complication due to insulin pump, followed by the appropriate diabetes mellitus code.

B. Use code 996.57, Mechanical complication due to insulin pump, as the principal code for an encounter due to an insulin pump malfunction resulting in an overdose of insulin, followed by code 962.3, Poisoning by insulin.

C. Use code 962.3, Poisoning by insulin first, followed by 996.57, Mechanical complication due to insulin pump.

D. Assign code 962.3, Poisoning by insulin first, followed by a secondary code for the diabetes.

146. **For aplastic anemia that is drug-induced or due to other external causes, the coder should:**

A. Use first a code to identify the anemia, followed by a secondary code to identify the substance.

B. Use first a code to identify the substance, followed by the anemia code.

C. Use a combination code for anemia caused by chemical substance, with the fifth digit representing the substance.

D. none of the above

147. **Subcategory 285.2, Anemia in chronic illness, has codes that may be used as secondary codes if treatment of the anemia is:**

A. the primary reasons for the encounter

B. related to another condition

C. not the primary reason for the encounter, but is included in the visit

D. not related to another condition

148. **Codes in chapter five include personality disorders, neuroses, psychoses, stress disorders, and sexual deviation conditions, and the fifth digit represents all of the following statuses EXCEPT:**

A. 0 – unspecified

B. 1 – continuous

C. 2 – episodic

D. 3 – chronic

149. **If delirium is due to a known physiological condition, the coder should:**

A. First code for Delirium due to known physiologic condition, followed by a secondary code for the underlying condition.

B. First code for the underling condition, followed by a secondary code for Delirium, NEC.

C. First code for Delirium NEC, followed by a secondary code for Unknown condition.

D. First code for the underlying condition, followed by a secondary code for Delirium due to known physiological condition.

150. **Avoid the use of the code for Central pain syndrome and Chronic pain syndrome unless:**

A. The provider has specifically documented this as a diagnosis.

B. The provider has mentioned this as a possible diagnosis but not listed it yet.

C. The patient reports he or she has this condition.

D. any of the above

151. **If the pain is not specified as acute or chronic, avoid use of codes from category 338, except for:**

A. post-thoracotomy pain

B. postoperative pain

C. neoplasm related pain

D. all of the above

152. **A patient is being treated for pain, which is related to a neoplasm. He is not receiving treatment for the neoplasm during this visit. The physician lists Pain *secondary to malignancy*, but she does not specify whether the pain is acute or chronic. What should the coder use as the first listed code?**

A. code 338.1

B. code 338.2

C. code 338.3

D. a code for unspecified pain

153. **Where is the hypertension table located in the ICD-9-CM manual?**

A. the Tabular List under *H*

B. the Alphabetic Index under *H*

C. the 400 Category under *H*

D. the 400 Category under *C*

154. **A patient has hypertensive chronic kidney disease, and is seen for this problem. The physician lists the condition as stage three. What should the coder do?**

A. Code from subcategory 402 and assign a fifth digit of 0.

B. Code from the subcategory 402 and assign a fifth digit of 1.

C. Code from the subcategory 403 and assign a fifth digit of 0.

D. Code from the subcategory 403 and assign a fifth digit of 1.

155. **A patient suffered a cerebrovascular event, but did not acquire any neurologic deficits. How would this be coded?**

A. with a code for cerebral infarction without residual deficits only

B. with a code for TIA only

C. with a combination code for cerebral infarction without residual deficits and TIA

D. with a code for TIA, followed by code for cerebral infarction without residual deficits

156. **A patient has peritonsillar abscess caused by Streptococcus. How would this be coded?**

A. first-listed code for the infectious agent, followed by secondary codes for upper respiratory infection and peritonsillar abscess

B. first-listed code for the infectious agent, followed by a secondary code for peritonsillar abscess

C. first-listed code for peritonsillar abscess, followed by a secondary code for the infectious agent

D. first-listed code for peritonsillar abscess, followed by a secondary code for the upper respiratory infection

157. **When coding a chronic condition for a patient who has a history of smoking, the coder would:**

A. First assign a code for the lung condition, followed by a secondary code for Personal history of nicotine dependence.

B. First assign a code for the lung condition, followed by a secondary code for Personal history of drug abuse.

C. First assign a code for Personal history of drug abuse, followed by a secondary code for the lung condition.

D. First assign a code for Personal history of nicotine dependence, followed by a secondary code for the lung condition.

158. **A patient is admitted with a respiratory condition related to a HIV infection, but he doesn't want his insurance to know about his HIV status. What should the coder do?**

   A. Explain to the patient that the HIV must be reported, and code the HIV disease first, followed by the code for the respiratory condition.

   B. Explain to the patient that the HIV must be reported, and code the respiratory condition first, followed by the code for the HIV disease.

   C. Code only for the respiratory condition.

   D. Code first Other infections disease, followed by a code for the respiratory condition.

159. **A patient with gingivitis has documented history of chewing tobacco use. The physician only lists *gingivitis* as the diagnosis. What should the coder do?**

   A. Code only for gingivitis.

   B. Code first for History of tobacco use or Tobacco use, followed by a secondary code for the gingivitis.

   C. Code first for the gingivitis, followed by a secondary code for History of tobacco use or Tobacco use.

   D. Code only for the use of tobacco.

160. **A patient comes in for stress incontinence. She has a long-standing history of a neurogenic bladder, COPD, and hypertension, but this is the first mention of incontinence. The physician lists only a diagnosis of stress incontinence for this encounter, and he does not treat any existing chronic conditions. How would this visit be coded?**

   A. The first-listed code would be Stress incontinence, followed by a secondary code for Neuromuscular dysfunction of bladder.

   B. The first-listed code would be Neuromuscular dysfunction of bladder, followed by a secondary code for Stress incontinence.

   C. The first-listed code would be Stress incontinence, followed by secondary codes for Neuromuscular dysfunction of bladder and Hypertension.

   D. The only listed code would be Stress incontinence.

161. **In chapter eleven, *Complications of Pregnancy, Childbirth, and the Puerperium*, the fifth digit denotes all of the following episodes of care EXCEPT:**

   A. 0 – Unknown

   B. 1 – Delivered, with or without antepartum condition

   C. 2 – Delivered with mention of postpartum complication

   D. 3 – Antepartum condition/complication

162. **When a pregnant woman has an injury or illness that is unrelated to her pregnancy, the coder should:**

   A. Code first with V22.2, Pregnant state incidental, followed by a secondary code for the illness or injury.

   B. Code only for the illness or injury, as the pregnancy is not related.

   C. Code first for the illness or injury, followed by a secondary code for the cause of the injury.

   D. Code first for the illness or injury, followed by the secondary code V22.2, Pregnant state incidental.

163. **If an abortion is documented as *incomplete*, what fifth digit would be added to the abortion code?**

   A. 0

   B. 1

   C. 2

   D. 3

164. **A pregnant woman, who has had type I diabetes since age seven, is pregnant. She is being seen in the prenatal clinic. How would the coder document this?**

   A. with a first-listed code from category 250, Diabetes mellitus

   B. with code 648.0x, Diabetes mellitus complicating pregnancy, followed by a secondary code from category 250, Diabetes mellitus

   C. with code 648.0x, Diabetes mellitus complicating pregnancy, followed by a secondary code from category 249, Secondary diabetes

   D. with code 648.0x only

165. **For coding skin change changes from exposure to radiation, the coder should:**

   A. First list a code for the type of skin condition, followed by a code to identify the source of ultraviolet radiation.

   B. First list a code for the ultraviolet radiation, followed by a code for the cause of skin injury.

   C. First list a code for the ultraviolet radiation, followed by a code for the type of skin condition.

   D. Only list a code for the skin condition, as the radiation exposure is incidental.

166. **A patient has a foreign body of the soft muscle tissue of the lower left leg. The physician only treats him to remove this object. How would this be coded?**

   A. with a first-listed code to identify the type of foreign body, followed by a secondary code for Foreign body of the soft muscle tissue

   B. with a first-listed code for Foreign body of the soft muscle tissue, followed by a secondary code for the type of foreign body

   C. with the code for Foreign body of the soft muscle tissue only

   D. with a code for the type of foreign body only

167. **A newborn infant is liveborn with a congenital anomaly and was born prematurely. How would this be coded?**

   A. with a first-listed code for Liveborn, followed by secondary codes for Low birth weight and immaturity status and a code to document the anomaly

   B. with a first-listed code to document the anomaly, followed by a secondary code for Low birth weight and immaturity status

   C. with a first-listed code for Low birth weight and immaturity status, followed by a secondary code for Liveborn

   D. with a first-listed code for Congenital anomaly, followed by a secondary code for Liveborn

168. **A patient was started on an antihistamine for allergies one week ago. Today, she is in the office for urinary retention. The physician's diagnosis is *Urinary retention, secondary to medication*. How would this be coded?**

   A. First list a code for urinary retention, followed by a secondary code to specify the drug.

   B. First list a code for urinary retention, followed by a secondary code to specify the allergies.

   C. First list a code to identify the drug, followed by a secondary code for urinary retention.

   D. Use a combination code for urinary retention and drug therapy.

169. **A patient received numerous second-degree burns to the face and hands, and one small first-degree burn to the left thigh. How would this be coded?**

   A. List Secondary-degree burns, multiple first, followed by a secondary code for the first-degree burn.

   B. First list a code for Multiple burns, followed by a secondary code for Burn, starting from the head and progressing down the body.

   C. Only use a code for Multiple burns, unspecified.

   D. First list a code for First-degree burn, followed by secondary codes for the second-degree burns.

170. **A patient has overdosed on Valium, but he survived the incident. He has a long-standing history of benzodiazepine abuse. How would this be coded?**

   A. Code first with the poisoning code, followed by a secondary code for the overdose and an additional code for drug abuse or dependence to the substance.

   B. Code first for the overdose, followed by an additional code for drug abuse or dependence to the substance.

   C. Code first for the overdose, followed by a secondary code for poisoning.

   D. Code first with the poisoning code, followed by a secondary code for drug abuse or dependence to the substance.

171. **The Supplementary Classification of Factors Influencing Health Status and Contact with Health Services (V01.0 - V91.99) involves all of the following circumstances for the use of V codes EXCEPT:**

   A. A person encounters the health services to act as an organ donor, to receive inoculations or health screenings, or to receive counseling.

   B. Issues or problems influence a person's health status but do not involve a current illness or injury.

   C. A person who has a resolved or resolving condition must use health services for aftercare.

   D. newborn prematurity status

172. **V Codes are status codes that:**

   A. are used when a patient is a carrier of a disease

   D. are used when a patient has the sequelae of a past condition

   C. are used for the presence of a mechanical device

   D. all of the above

173. **When is it appropriate to use code V45.88, Do not resuscitate status?**

   A. when it is documented by a nurse

   B. when it is documented by the provider

   C. when it is reported by the patient

   D. it is never appropriate to use this code

174. **What code would be used for a patient who comes in only to have a prothrombin time blood test for long-standing use of Coumadin?**

   A. V56.6x, Long-term (current) drug use

   B. V58.7x, Long-term (current) drug use

   C. V58.8x, Long-term (current) drug use

   D. V58.9x, Long-term (current) drug use

175. **Family history codes are used to show:**

   A. that a patient has potential risk for contracting a disease, disorder, or condition because a patient has a family member(s) who could have died due to that disease, disorder, or condition

   B. that a patient has minimal risk for contracting a disease, disorder, or condition because a patient has a family member(s) has or had a particular disease

   C. that a patient has no risk for contracting a disease, disorder, or condition because a patient has a family member(s) who never had that particular disease

   D. that a patient has a high risk for contracting a disease, disorder, or condition because a patient has a family member(s) who has or had a particular disease

176. **An E code is:**

   A. never the first-listed diagnosis

   B. used to indicate a family history of a disease, condition, or illness

   C. used for the initial encounter of an injury, poisoning, or adverse effect of drugs, as well as for subsequent treatment

   D. all of the above

177. **In the ICD-10-CM manual, which codes represent factors that influence health status and contact with health services?**

   A. E codes

   B. V codes

   C. Y codes

   D. Z codes

178. **A terrorism event resulted in a bus accident. A patient on the bus is brought into the emergency department for a fracture to the right tibia. The physician lists a diagnosis of Fracture to the right tibia, secondary to bus accident. You know to use a code for the terrorism event additionally. In what order would the codes be listed?**

A. E code for the terrorism event, followed by a secondary code for the fracture and a tertiary code for the bus accident

B. E code for the bus accident, followed by a secondary code for the fracture and a tertiary code for the terrorism event

C. a first-listed code for the fracture, followed by a secondary code for the bus accident and a tertiary code for the terrorism event

D. a first-listed code for the fracture, followed by a secondary code for the terrorism event and a tertiary code for the bus accident

179. **With ICD-10-CM, the letter _x_ is used as:**

A. the third character dummy placeholder for many six-character codes

B. the fourth character dummy placeholder for many six-character codes

C. the fifth character dummy placeholder for many six-character codes

D. the sixth character dummy placeholder for many six-character codes

180. **ICD-10-CM codes:**

A. have three- to seven-digit alphanumeric codes

B. describe diseases, illnesses, injuries, procedures, and signs/symptoms

C. have one or more definitions

D. all of the above

181. **The ICD-10-CM classification system offers many benefits, such as improved:**

A. strategic planning and healthcare delivery system design

B. provider and healthcare staff performance

C. ability to track provider spending

D. all of the above

182. **Of the following, which is true concerning the ICD-9-CM and ICD-10-CM?**

A. The ICD-9-CM system uses a Tabular List and Alphabetic Index, whereas the ICD-10-CM uses an Alphabetic List and a Tabular Index.

B. Both systems use _unspecified_ and _not otherwise specified_ codes when a more specific code is not available.

C. Both Tabular lists are structured exactly the same.

D. Codes are looked up the same way in both systems, with diagnostic terms from the Tabular List and verified code number from the Alphabetic Index.

183. **Which of the following is NOT a difference between ICD-9-CM and ICD-10-CM?**

A. In the ICD-9-CM, codes are invalid if they are missing an applicable character, whereas in the ICD-10-CM they would be valid.

B. ICD-10-CM codes are more complete, so the coder does not need to refer back to the category or subcategory level.

C. ICD-10-CM uses a dummy placeholder _x_ to allow for future expansion and to fill out empty characters when there are fewer than six, or when a seventh character applies.

D. ICD-10-CM codes are longer than ICD-9-CM codes, with up to seven characters.

184. **What notes in ICD-10-CM advise the coder to look somewhere else before assigning a code?**

   A. tabular notes

   B. excludes notes

   C. category notes

   D. cross-reference notes

185. **What ICD-10-CM word or phrase means that there is a casual relationship between two conditions?**

   A. and

   B. with

   C. due to

   D. because of

186. **HCPCS stands for:**

   A. healthcare common procedure code set

   B. health common problem coding set

   C. healthcare common procedure coding system

   D. health core problem coding system

187. **All of the following nonphysician services are included in the HCPCS EXCEPT:**

   A. urinary catheter supplies

   B. syringes and needles

   C. bedside commodes

   D. holter monitors

188. **A service related to Temporary Hospital Outpatient Prospective Payment System would be found in which code category?**

   A. A

   B. B

   C. C

   D. G

189. **If a patient has a procedure for an injury to the left upper eyelid, what HCPSC modifier could you use?**

   A. −LT

   B. −E1

   C. − F1

   D. none of the above

190. **Who is covered by Medicare insurance?**

   A. low-income children

   B. disabled veterans

   C. people under the age of sixty-five years

   D. none of the above

191. **Which segment of Medicare covers the Prescription Drug Plan (PDP), which includes Medicare Advantage Plans (MA-PDs), Private Prescription Drug Plans (PDPs), and premiums paid by the beneficiary?**

   A. part A

   B. part B

   C. part C

   D. part D

192. **What was the purpose of the National Correct Coding Initiative (NCCI)?**

   A. to promote national coding methods and control improper coding and reimbursement

   B. to ensure quality of patient care

   C. to see that Medicare only pays for necessary and reasonable services

   D. to protect the Medicare beneficiaries

193. **What Medicare payment reform established a fee schedule, which allows payment of eighty percent?**

   A. the National Fee Schedule (NFS)

   B. the Resource-Based Relative Value Scale (RBRVS)

   C. the Relative Value Unit (RVU)

   D. the Current Procedure Terminology (CPT)

194. **CPT codes are updated and published by:**

    A. the Centers for Disease Control and Prevention (CDC)

    B. the Center for Medicare and Medicaid Services (CMS)

    C. the AMA

    D. the AHA

195. **Codes used for supplemental tracking and performance measurement are:**

    A. category I codes

    B. category II codes

    C. category III codes

    D. category IV codes

196. **Level I CPT and HCPCS codes contain modifiers, which are two-digit codes that can be:**

    A. numeric

    B. alphanumeric

    C. alpha

    D. all of the above

197. **Which modifier indicates that the anesthesia services required more time and supplies than usual?**

    A. -22

    B. -23

    C. -24

    D. -25

198. **What does modifier -51 indicate?**

    A. that the physician was involved

    B. that a procedure was performed on organs that are bilateral, such as kidneys or lungs

    C. that the same procedure was performed on different sites, that multiple procedures were performed, or that the procedure was performed multiple times

    D. that the procedure was started but then stopped for some reason

199. **Which modifier is used when the services need more than one modifier?**

    A. -90

    B. -91

    C. -92

    D. -99

200. **When selecting evaluation and management (E/M) codes, the coder must consider the place of service, type of service, and patient status. The patient status can be all of the following EXCEPT:**

    A. inpatient

    B. outpatient

    C. new patient

    D. observation patient

201. **The level of E/M service is based upon:**

    A. effort required

    B. time spent with the patient

    C. skill necessary to perform the service

    D. all of the above

202. **Which of the following is not one of the three elements of medical decision making?**

    A. the problem addressed

    B. the patient status

    C. the data reviewed

    D. the level of risk

203. **The number of diagnoses and management options is multiple, the risk of death or complications is moderate, and the amount of complexity is also moderate with this type of medical decision making:**

    A. straightforward

    B. low-complexity

    C. moderate-complexity

    D. high-complexity

204. **Which CPT codes are used for patients not ill enough to be admitted, but those that require monitoring?**

   A. Initial Observation Care (99218-99220)

   B. Established Patient (99211-99215)

   C. Consultation Services (99241-99255)

   D. Hospital Inpatient Services (99221-99239)

205. **Care Plan Oversight Services (99374-99380) codes are used to report:**

   A. physician supervision of patient care in the home health agency setting

   B. physician supervision of patient care in the hospice setting

   C. both A and B

   D. neither A nor B

206. **All of the following are methods of anesthesia EXCEPT:**

   A. epidural

   B. general

   C. local

   D. endobronchial

207. **The anesthesia formula for payment is:**

   A. (T x B x M) + Conversion Factor

   B. (B + T + M) x Conversion Factor

   C. (B – T) x Conversion Factor

   D. none of the above

208. **How many radiology subsections are in the CPT system?**

   A. 4

   B. 5

   C. 7

   D. 10

209. **Which of the following is NOT a component of the radiology section of CPT?**

   A. traditional component

   B. technical component

   C. professional component

   D. global component

210. **Which radiology codes of CPT are used for various placement of radioactive material into the body, as well as measurement of emissions?**

   A. Diagnostic Radiology (70010 - 76499)

   B. Radiologic Guidance (77001 - 77032)

   C. Radiation Oncology (77261 - 77799)

   D. Nuclear Medicine (78000 - 79999)

211. **Which CPT codes are used for tests on urine, blood, breath, feces, and sputum?**

   A. Evocative and Suppression Testing (80400 - 80440)

   B. Molecular Pathology (81200 - 81406)

   C. Chemistry (82000 - 84999)

   D. Hematology and Coagulation (85002 - 85999)

212. **Cytogenetic Studies (88230 - 88299) CPT codes are used for:**

   A. collection, processing, and typing of blood

   B. specimen testing on tissue samples (biopsies)

   C. various microscopic tests to identify organisms

   D. autopsies

213. **Bacteria that cause illness are made nontoxic, and these immunizations are called:**

   A. toxins

   B. toxoid

   C. toxicology

   D. toximetry

214. **Pulmonary (94002 - 94799) CPT codes are used for:**

   A. ventilation diagnostic tests

   B. ventilation management therapy

   C. both A and B

   D. neither A nor B

215. **Dialysis (90935 - 90999) CPT codes are used for:**

   A. hemodialysis

   B. ESRD nurse services

   C. both A and B

   D. neither A nor B

216. **Ophthalmology CPT E/M eye codes are used for:**

   A. only right eye services

   B. only left eye services

   C. only eyelid services

   D. none of the above

217. **Allergy and Clinical Immunology (95004 - 95199) CPT codes are used for:**

   A. allergy diagnoses

   B. immunology diagnoses

   C. both A and B

   D. neither A nor B

218. **The biopsy subsection (11100-11101) codes are used for excision of:**

   A. a small piece of skin

   B. a small piece of subcutaneous tissue

   C. a small piece of mucous membrane tissue

   D. all of the above.

219. **With an incision and drainage code (10400 – 10180), what is cutting into the skin considered?**

   A. aspiration

   B. insertion

   C. lancing

   D. all of the above

220. **You are coding for removal of a benign skin lesion, using a code from subsection 11400-11646. What would be included in this procedure?**

   A. lesion removal

   B. local anesthesia

   C. simple closure

   D. all of the above

221. **What type of surgical fracture repair occurs by insertion of devices through the skin or other site?**

   A. percutaneous

   B. closed

   C. open

   D. all of the above

222. **Which CPT surgical procedure codes are used for aspirations, injections, insertions, removals, applications, and adjustments, as well as for various therapeutic sinus tract injections, catheter placement, and antibiotics injections?**

   A. Excision (20150-20251)

   B. Wound Exploration (20100-20103)

   C. Introduction or Removal (20500-20689)

   D. External Fixation (20690-20697)

223. **When are Casting and Strapping (20939-29799) codes NOT used?**

   A. when the application of a cast or strap is included in the surgical procedure

   B. when there is a subsequent cast application necessary

   C. when a cast application is the treatment for a fracture

   D. when the visit is only for application of an ace bandage

224. **The CPT respiratory system subsection includes procedures and services related to the nose, sinuses, larynx, bronchus, trachea, pleura, and lungs, and the codes are divided by:**

   A. site

   B. incision

   C. excision

   D. all of the above

225. **When is diagnostic endoscopy included in the surgical endoscopy CPT code?**

   A. always

   B. sometimes

   C. never

   D. with exceptions

226. **If the endoscopy procedure begins at the mouth and ends at the bronchial tube, code for:**

   A. bronchial tube

   B. bronchial tube = full extent

   C. bronchial tube = partial extent

   D. bronchial tube = unspecified

227. **The nose incision codes include drain or gauze insertion, as well as removal of lesion or growth. Excision codes in this subsection are intranasal biopsy codes, as well as polyp and turbinate excision and resection. When both sides are involved, use modifier:**

   A. -TC

   B. -50

   C. -51

   D. -52

228. **Which of the following is an example of a noninvasive cardiovascular procedure?**

   A. incision of the valve

   B. electrocardiogram

   C. catheter insertion

   D. excision of lesion

229. **Cardiography (93000 - 93278) codes are used for:**

   A. stress tests

   B. holter monitors

   C. electrocardiograms

   D. all of the above

230. **What CPT codes are used for various arterial and venous grafting procedures?**

   A. Heart and Pericardium (33010 – 33999)

   B. Arteries and Veins (34001 – 37799)

   C. Venous and Arterial Grafting (33517 - 33536)

   D. Endovascular Repair of Descending Aorta (33830 - 33891)

231. **A radical lymphadnectomy involves removal of aortic and splenic lymph nodes, as well as the surrounding tissue. When this procedure is done along with a major procedure, it should:**

   A. be bundled

   B. be coded separately

   C. be included

   D. be omitted

232. **Regarding the hemic and lymphatic systems section, general (38204 - 38242) codes are used for:**

   A. bone marrow biopsy

   B. bone marrow harvesting

   C. bone marrow preservation

   D. all of the above

233. **Which type of digestive system scope procedure is used to examine and treat the esophagus and past the diaphragm?**

   A. esophagoscopy

   B. esophagogastroscopy

   C. esophagogastroduodenoscopy

   D. signmoidoscopy

234. **Hernia (49491 - 49659) CPT codes are used for various hernia repairs and surgical procedures related to hernias, and they are divided by:**

   A. type

   B. patient

   C. presentation

   D. all of the above

235. **Kidney (50010 - 50593) CPT codes are:**

   A. unilateral

   B. bilateral

   C. both A and B

   D. neither A nor B

236. **These CPT codes are used for transurethral resection of the prostate (TURP) procedures:**

   A. Bladder (51020 - 52700)

   B. Vesical Neck and Prostate (52400-52700)

   C. both A and B

   D. neither A nor B

237. **Maternity Care and Delivery (59000 - 59899) CPT codes are used for:**

   A. cesarean section

   B. biopsies of the female genital system

   C. biopsies of a newborn

   D. all of the above

238. **Male Genital System (54000 - 55899) destruction codes are divided by:**

   A. extent of the procedure

   B. number of physicians

   C. type of instrument

   D. all of the above

239. **Female Genital System (56405 - 58770) destruction codes are divided by:**

   A. extent of procedure

   B. type of procedure

   C. both A and B

   D. neither A nor B

240. **These CPT codes are used for various procedures related to the thyroid, parathyroid, thymus, and adrenal glands:**

   A. Endocrine System (60000 - 60699)

   B. Eye and Adnexa (65091 - 68899)

   C. Nervous System (61000 - 64999)

   D. Auditory System (69000 - 69979)

1.   C. 18%

The integument is the skin, which makes up about eighteen percent of the body's weight.

2.   D. all of the above

Skin is necessary to protect the body from the invasion of microorganisms, and to regulate body temperature and manufacture vitamins.

3.   A. epidermis

The epidermis is the outermost layer, and it contains four sections, called stratum. The stratum basale is the deepest section. The second skin layer is the dermis, which contains two sections: papillare and reticulare. Also in the dermis are nerves, blood vessels, nails, glands, hair, and connective tissue. The subcutaneous tissue is also called the hypo-dermis, which contains connective tissue and fat tissue, and connects the skin to underlying muscle.

4.   B. dermis

The sebaceous (oil) glands are in the dermis, and they secrete oil (sebum) that lubricates the skin and hair. The sudoriferous (sweat) glands are also in the dermis, and they secrete salty water to cool the body.

5.   B. lack of or decreased sweat

Hyperhydrosis is too much or increased sweat, and anhidrosis is lack of or decreased sweat.

6.   C. lipoma

Adipose tissue is also called fat tissue. A hematoma is a localized collection of blood. A steatoma is a fatty mass of the sebaceous gland. A lipoma is a simple, fatty mass of the skin.

7.   A. atopic

Atopic dermatitis (eczema) is caused by irritants or allergens that activate mast cells, eosinophils, T lymphocytes, and monocytes. It occurs in those with a family history of the condition, as well as asthma and allergies, and it is more common in infants and children.

8.   C. keloid

A macule is a flat skin mole or freckle. A papule is a solid, elevated one centimeter skin lesion, such as a wart, mole, or lichen planus. A nodule is a solid, elevated, one-to-two centimeter skin lesion , such as a lipoma, lymph node, or erythema nodusum. A keloid is an irregular shaped, elevated scar that occurs from excessive collagen in the corneum during tissue repair.

9.   A. skin cracks, such as athlete's foot, or cracks in the corners of the mouth

A wheal is temporary, localized skin elevation, such as an insect bite or allergic reaction. Atrophy is loss of a portion of the skin, which is a physiologic response to aging. A crust is dried skin exudate (scab).

10.   C. pityriasis rosea

Stasis dermatitis is associated with phlebitis, var-icosities, and vascular trauma, and it begins with pruritus and erythema and progresses to hyperpig-mentation, scaling, petechia, and ulcerated lesions. The cause of psoriasis is unknown, but thought to be caused from immunologic disorder, a trig-gering agent, or biochemical alterations. It results in well-demarcated plaques and scaly, flaky, and inflamed skin. The cause of pityriasis is unknown, but it is associated with a primary lesion called a *herald patch*, which is a salmon-colored, circular three-to-four centimeter lesion. Secondary lesions are oval, reddened, and itchy, occurring around days fourteen to twenty-one.

11. C. keratoacanthoma

Three common benign skin tumors are seborrheic keratosis, actinic keratosis, and keratoacanthoma, which is a scaly pigmented patch that occurs in hair follicles. Basal cell carcinoma is a shiny, reddened cancerous lesion that is slow-growing in deep skin layers and basal cells. Melanoma is a malignant lesion that originates in the melanocytes. Kaposi's sarcoma is a rare form of vascular skin cancer that is associated with human immunodeficiency virus/acquired immunodeficiency syndrome (HIV/AIDS).

12. A. cellulitis

Folliculitis is an infection of the hair follicles that results in erythema and pustules. A furuncle is a boil caused by an infected hair follicle. Impetigo is a highly contagious pyoderma caused by Staphylococcus.

13. D. all of the above

Herpes simplex virus (HSV) (cold sores) are red blisters near the lips and mouth (type 1 HSV-1) or genital area (type 2 HSV-2). Herpes zoster (shingles) is red blisters that burn and sting and occur on an area of skin innervated by one of the cranial nerves.

14. D. pedis

Tinea capitis occurs on the scalp. Tinea corporis (ringworm) can occur anywhere on the body. Tinea manis occurs on the hands. Tinea unguium occurs on the nails. Tinea pedis occurs on the feet.

15. C. macules

The symptoms of acne vulgaris include blackheads, whiteheads, pustules, cysts, and papules.

16. D. 206

The musculoskeletal system is comprised of the bony skeleton, skeletal muscles, cardiac muscles, and smooth muscles. There also are 206 bones, as well as cartilage and ligaments. The muscular system protects the organs, produces heat, assists with movement, and forms body shape.

17. B. scapula

The long bones are tubular bones, including the femur, tibia, fibula, humerus, ulna, and radius bones. The short bones are cuboidal bones, such as the carpals and tarsals. The flat bones are thin and flat, such as the skull, sternum, and scapula. Seasamoid bones are rounded, such as the patella. The zygoma and vertebra are irregular bones.

18. B. ethmoid

The axial skeleton includes the skull, hyoid bone, vertebral column, sacrum, ribs, and sternum. The skull bones include the frontal (forehead), parietal (sides), temporal (lower sides), occipital (posterior), sphenoid (floor), ethmoid (between eye orbits and nasal cavity) styloid process (below ear), and zygomatic process (cheek). The middle ear bones include the malleus (hammer), incus (anvil), and stapes (stirrup).

19. C. zygomatic

The facial bones include the maxilla (upper jaw), nasal (bridge of nose), zygomatic (cheekbone), mandible (jaw), lacrimal (near eye orbits), vomer (nasal septum), palate (between oral and nasal cavities), and nasal conchae (turbinates).

20. D. ilium

The pelvis contains the ilium (upper part), ischium (posterior part), pubis (anterior part), and pubis symphysis (cartilage of the pubic bones).

21. B. ulna

The two lower arm bones are the radius (larger) and ulna (smaller). The humerus is the upper arm bone, and the talus is the ankle bone.

22. A. visceral

Skeletal tissue is the striated tissue that attaches to bones. Cardiac tissue is heart muscle that is both striated and smooth. Visceral tissue is smooth tissue that lines the bowel, blood vessels, and urethra.

23. C. sternocleidomastoid – grates teeth

The pterygolds muscle grates the teeth, and the sternocleidomastoid muscle flexes the head. Choices A., B., and C. are matched correctly.

24. A. chondral

Chondral pertains to cartilage. A ganglion is a knot-like cyst. Articular pertains to a joint, and a bursa is a joint sac.

25. C. open fracture

A closed fracture is a simple break where the bone does not penetrate the skin. A complete fracture is a break where the bone is in two pieces or more (oblique, spiral, linear, and transverse). An incomplete fracture is a break where the bone is not broken in two or more pieces (greenstick, torus, stress, and bowing).

26. B. bacteria

Osteomyelitis is a bone infection caused by bacteria. Osteoporosis is decreased bone mass and density that occurs due to malabsorption of calcium and other substances and is associated with advancing age. Osteomalacia is softening of adult bones.

27. C. gouty arthritis

Spina bifida is a congenital abnormality where vertebrae do not close around the spinal cord. Septic arthritis is an infectious process that generally affects a single joint. Ankylosing spondylosis is a progressive inflammatory disease that affects vertebral joints. Gouty arthritis is a joint condition caused by uric acid accumulation.

28. C. muscular dystrophy

Muscular dystrophy is a progressive degenerative muscle disorder that has a genetic predisposition. Fibromyalgia is a condition that involves generalized pain and aching that often affects middle-aged women. Polymyositis is generalized muscle inflammation that causes weakness.

29. A. chondroblastoma

Both chondroblastoma and osteoma are benign. Multiple myeloma is malignant cells in the soft tissue and skeleton. Rhabdomyosarcoma is an aggressive and invasive malignant carcinoma. Osteosarcoma is a malignant tumor of the long bones.

30. B. rheumatoid arthritis

Osteoarthritis is degeneration and inflammation of the joint. Rheumatoid arthritis is progressive auto-immune disease that affects the connective tissues and joints. Septic arthritis is an infectious process that generally affects a single joint. Gouty arthritis is caused by excessive uric acid in the joints.

31. A. turbinates

The upper respiratory tract includes the nose, sinuses, turbinates, pharynx, and larynx. The lower respiratory tract involves the trachea, bronchial tree, and lungs. Both upper and lower structures supply oxygen and rid the body of carbon dioxide.

32. B. larynx

The turbinates are also called conchae, and they are the bones of the nose that are inferior, middle, or superior. The pharynx is the throat passageway for air and food. The larynx is the voicebox that contains vocal cords and cartilage.

33. B. cyanosis

Asphyxia is lack of oxygen, orthopnea is shortness of breath when lying flat, and tachypnea is rapid respirations. When the skin and/or lips get blue, this is called cyanosis.

34. B. epitaxis

The medical term for nose bleed is epitaxis. Atelectasis is incomplete lung expansion, cyanosis is bluish discoloration of the skin and lips, and pleuritis is inflammation of the pleura.

35. A. The patient is coughing up blood and has drainage from the nose.

Hemoptysis is coughing up blood, and rhinorrhea is drainage from the nose.

36. D. adult respiratory distress syndrome (ARDS)

Acute respiratory failure is a condition of inadequate gas exchange that results in hypoxemia. Respiratory acidosis is excess retention of carbon dioxide leads to low level of pH. A pneumothorax is a condition where air collects in the pleural cavity. ARDS is an acute injury to the alveolo-capillary membrane that results in atelectasis and edema.

37. D. all of the above

With bronchiectasis, the chronic dilation of the bronchi can be cylindrical, varicose, cystic, or sacular.

38. D. pus

A pulmonary embolism is caused by occlusion due to air, blood clot, or tissue that lodges in a pulmonary artery.

39. A. the pleural space

Empyema is infectious pleura effusion where there is pus in the pleural space.

40. C. pneumonia

Pneumonia is an acute condition where there is inflammation of the lungs due to aspiration, bacteria, protozoa, viruses, fungi, or chlamydia. COPD is a chronic, irreversible obstruction of the lungs that decreases expiration. Chronic bronchitis is a form of COPD that causes dyspnea, wheezing, and productive cough. Emphysema is another form of COPD that causes enlargement of alveoli and loss of lung elasticity.

41. B. hypercapnia

Hypercapnia is increased carbon dioxide in the arterial blood caused by poor alveoli ventilation. Hypoxemia is reduced oxygenation of the arterial blood. Bronchiectasis is chronic dilation of the bronchi that can be cylindrical, varicose, cystic, or sacular. Bronchiolitis is obstruction of the bronchioles caused by inflammation from a viral pathogen, such as RSV.

42. B. It goes down.

With respiratory acidosis, there is excess retention of carbon dioxide, which leads to a low level of pH.

43. C. coal, asbestos, or fiberglass

With pneumoconiosis, coal, asbestos, or fiberglass particles invade the tissue.

44. C. pleurisy

Pneumoconiosis is caused by particles in the lung tissue. PE is caused by occlusion due to air, blood clot, or tissue that lodges in a pulmonary artery. COPD is caused by smoking. Pleurisy, also called pleuritis, is inflammation of the pleura due to an upper respiratory infection.

45. C. both A and B

The upper respiratory tract includes the nose, sinuses, turbinates, pharynx, and larynx. The lower respiratory tract involves the trachea, bronchial tree, and lungs. All of these structures supply oxygen and rid the body of carbon dioxide.

46. B. the blood

The cardiovascular system consists of the heart, blood, and blood vessels. The vessels carry blood throughout the body, the heart pumps the blood and allows for oxygen—carbon dioxide exchange, and the blood transports nutrients and hormones.

47. C. 91%

Plasma is the liquid part of the blood that is ninety-one percent water.

48. A. plasma

The liquid part of the blood is called plasma (mostly water), and the cellular part contains leukocytes (WBCs), erythrocytes (red blood cells or RBCs), and thrombocytes (platelets).

49. B. arteries

The vessels transport blood and carry away cellular waste and carbon dioxide. The arteries lead away from the heart and branch into arterioles. The veins lead to the heart and branch into venules. The capillaries connect between arterioles and venules.

50. C. four

The two upper chambers are the right atrium and left atrium. The two lower chambers are the right ventricle and the left ventricle.

51. C. tricuspid

The tricuspid valve lies between the right atrium and the right ventricle. The pulmonary valve lies between the pulmonary artery and the right ventricle. The aortic valve lies between the aorta and the left ventricle. The bicuspid (mitral) valve lies between the left atrium and the left ventricle.

52. B. over the heart

Epicardial means over the heart.

53. C. RBCs

Hemolysis is RBC breakdown.

54. D. plaque

An atherectomy is removal of plaque from an artery, which is done by a percutaneous method. An embolectomy is removal of an embolism or blockage from a vessel. A thoracostomy is a procedure where incisions are made into the chest wall to insert a chest tube, to drain pus. Angioplasty is a procedure used to dilate a vessel opening.

55. D. trauma

CAD risk factors include advanced age, family history, hyperlipidemia, hypertension, cigarette smoking, diabetes, and obesity.

56. B. myocardial infarction (MI)

Coronary artery disease is also called ischemic heart disease. Hypertension is also called high blood pressure. An aneurysm is a dilated blood vessel. MI results from myocardial ischemia and is also called a heart attack. The symptoms of this are crushing chest pain and hypotension.

57. D. ischemia

A thrombus is also called a blood clot, and it is caused by infection, inflammation, low blood pressure, obstruction, and atherosclerosis.

58. A. dizziness, blurred vision, and syncope

Hypotension is also called low blood pressure. It is caused by a drop in both systolic and diastolic arterial blood pressure and insufficient oxygen in blood. The symptoms include dizziness, blurred vision, and syncope (fainting).

59. B. Buerger's disease

PAD is also called Buerger's disease. It is inflammation of the peripheral arteries creating vasospasms, which is caused by atherosclerosis.

60. C. cardiomyopathies

Cardiomyopathies are a group of cardiac diseases that affect the myocardium. They are caused by idiopathic or existing conditions. Types include dilated cardiomyopathy, hypertrophic cardiomyopathy, and restrictive cardiomyopathy.

61. A. cancer cells

An embolism is a mass that enters the bloodstream. Types include air, fat, bacteria, cancer cells, foreign substances, thrombus, and amniotic fluid.

62. A. leg pain and swelling

Varicose veins are also called varicosities, which occur when blood pools in the veins and distends them. The symptoms include leg swelling, leg pain, leg fatigue, and ulcerations.

63. D. blood clots

Infective endocarditis is inflammation of the inner lining of the heart that causes permanent heart valve damage. Causes include bacteria, viruses, fungi, or parasites.

64. B. atrial fibrillation

Atrial fibrillation is rapid, erratic contractions of the heart. Atrial flutter is rapid regular heart contractions. Ventricular fibrillation is a life-threatening rhythm of random electrical impulses through the ventricles. Asystole is absence of heart rhythm.

65. C. three

Pericarditis is inflammation of the heart pericardium. The types include acute, pericardial effusion, and constrictive.

66. C. both A and B

The female reproductive system protects the fertilized ovum (egg) for the nine-month gestation period. The external structures enhance sexual stimulation and protect the body from foreign materials. The internal structures produce and release the ovum.

67. B. myometrium

The uterus is a muscular organ with three layers: endometrium (inner mucosa), myometrium (middle layer), and perimetrium (outer layer). The vulva is the external genitalia.

68. B. endometrium repair

The phases of menstruation include: the proliferation phase (from day one through day five), the endometrium repair (from day six through day twelve), the secretory phase (from day thirteen through day fourteen), and premenstruation (from day fifteen through day twenty-eight).

69. C. 266

Human gestation is approximately nine months, or 266 days.

70. C. twenty-eight

Trimesters – first (LMP – twelve weeks), second (thirteen – twenty-seven weeks), and third (twenty-eight weeks – EDD).

71. B. occurred outside the uterus

An ectopic pregnancy is one that occurs outside the uterus, usually in the fallopian tube. Termination of pregnancy is abortion, and multipara is more than one pregnancy.

72. D. perineum

A cystocele is a herniation of the bladder into the vagina. Antepartum is the time before childbirth. Introitus is the opening of the vagina. The perineum is the region between the vagina and anus.

73. A. primary dysmenorrhea

Primary dysmenorrhea is pelvic cramping that occurs at the beginning of menstruation. Secondary dysmenorrhea is painful menstruation due to an underlying condition, such as endometriosis, tumors, or polyps. Menorrhagia is an increase in bleeding amount and duration of flow.

74. D. Menstruation has never occurred.

Primary amenorrhea is a genetic disorder where menstruation has never occurred.

75. B. certain foods

Secondary amenorrhea is where menstruation ceases for three cycles or six months. Known causes include stress, tumors, eating disorders, and strenuous exercise.

76. D. menometorrhagia

Metorrhagia is bleeding between cycles, menorrhagia is an increase in bleeding amount and duration of flow, and hypomenorrhea is light or spotty flow.

77. D. candidiasis

Candidiasis, also called a yeast infection, causes white curd-like discharge, pain with sex, and dysuria.

78. C. condylomata

Condylomata acuminata (genital warts) is caused by the human papillomavirus. Symptoms include polyps, growths, and warty lesions.

79. C. eclampsia

Amenorrhea means lack of menstruation. Placenta previa is when the cervical opening is obstructed by placenta. Adenomyosis is an enlarged uterus, abnormal menstrual bleeding, and pain. Eclampsia is the condition of pregnancy characterized by edema, hypertension, and proteinuria.

80. B. trichomoniasis

Candidasis is caused by a fungus. Chlamydia and gonorrhea are both caused by bacteria. Trichomoniasis is caused by the *trichomonas vaginalis* protozoan. Symptoms include colored vaginal or penis discharge and dysuria.

81. C. submucus

Terms include: beneath the endometrium (submucus), beneath the serosa (subserosa), and in the muscle wall (intramural).

82. D. testes

The testes, or gonads, produce sperm, as well as testosterone. The prostate gland produces seminal fluid and activates sperm. The seminal vesicles transport sperm from the testes to the exterior. The bulbourethral gland secretes a tiny amount of seminal fluid.

83. C. vas deferens

The vas deferens is the tubular structure at the end of the epididymis.

84. A. orchiopexy

Orchiopexy is the surgical procedure to lower undescended testis. A prostatotomy is an incision to the prostate. TURP is a surgical procedure performed by way of cystoscopy to remove some or all of the prostate gland. A vasectomy is removal of a portion of the vas deferens. A vesiculotomy is an incision into the seminal vesicle.

85. D. testicular torsion

Testicular torsion is twisting of the testes, which is caused by congenital abnormal development of the tunica vaginalis and spermatic cord or from trauma. Symptoms include severe pain, nausea, vomiting, edema, and fever.

86. A. scrotal pain

Epididymitis is inflammation of the epididymis. Causes include trauma, injury, or infection. Symptoms include scrotal pain, swelling, redness, and hydrocele.

87. C. corpora cavernosa

The epididymis is the structure that holds the sperm, located on the upper portion of the testes. Chordee is a condition where the penis is injured. A varicocele is swelling of a scrotal vein. Corpora cavernosa are the two cavities of the penis.

88. B. erispadias

A testicular torsion is twisting of the testes. Hypospadias is when the urethral opening occurs on the ventral side of the penis. Phimosis is where the foreskin is constricted and cannot be retracted. Erispadias is where the urethral meatus is mislocated to the dorsal side of penis.

89. B. prostatitis

Benign prostatic hypertrophy (BPH) is an enlarged prostate gland. Symptoms include nocturia, incontinence, hesitancy, and urinary urgency. Prostatitis is caused by E. coli and other bacteria, and symptoms include fever, low back pain, perineal pain, dysuria, suprapubic tenderness, and urinary tract infection (UTI).

90.   D. BPH

BPH is caused by increased levels of hormones and fibrous nodules. Phimosis is caused by chronic infection or poor hygiene. Urethritis is caused from bacterial organisms, and prostatitis is caused from E.coli and other bacteria.

91.   B. paraphimosis

With phimosis, the foreskin is constricted and cannot be retracted, and this condition is caused by chronic infection and poor hygiene. With paraphimosis, the foreskin is constricted and retracted over the penis.

92.   D. pancreas

The urinary system includes the kidneys, ureters, urinary bladder, and urethra. These structures work together to remove metabolic waste materials from the body, such as uric acid, urea, nitrogenous waste, and creatinine. The urinary system also maintains electrolyte balance and assists the liver in body detoxification.

93.   D. cortex

Kidneys are the two organs that control pH balance (acid/base), secrete berenin, vitamin D, and erythropoietin, and stimulate RBC production. The cortex is the outer layer of the kidney, the medullar is the inner portion of the kidney, the hilum is the middle section of the kidney, and the papilla is the inner part of the pyramids.

94.   D. urethroplasty

Cystoplasty is surgical reconstruction of bladder. Cystoscopy is the use of a scope to view the bladder. Ureterectomy is surgical removal of a ureter. Urethroplasy is the surgical repair of the urethra.

95.   A. interrenal

Acute renal failure is the sudden onset of kidney failure. Types include prerenal, intrarenal, and postrenal.

96.   B. hypertension

The symptoms of acute pyelonephritis are fever, groin pain, flank pain, dysuria, nausea, pyuria, and nocturia. The symptoms of chronic pyelonephritis are hypertension, dysuria, flank pain, and frequent urination.

97.   C. APSAGN

APSAGN is inflammation of the glomerulus caused by Streptococcus. Symptoms include back pain, flank pain, fatigue, headache, nausea, oliguria, elevated blood pressure, and malaise.

98.   D. PKD

APSAGN is caused by Streptococcus. BPH is a condition of the prostate, not the kidney. COPD is a lung condition. PKD is a genetic kidney condition.

99.   D. all of the above

The digestive system includes the gastrointestinal tract and various accessory organs. This system functions include absorption, digestion, and elimination. The GI tract is regulated by a complex series of hormonal, neural, and local control systems.

100. C. 32

Adults have thirty-two permanent teeth.

101. B. gallbladder

The stomach is the digestive organ that contains the fundus (upper region), body (middle region), and antrum (lower region). The liver is the digestive organ that produces bile and breaks down wastes. The gallbladder is a small organ that stores bile. The pancreas is the digestive organ that produces enzymes for digestion.

102. D. proctosigmoidoscopy

Cholecystectomy involves surgical removal of the gallbladder. Colonoscopy is a fiberscopic examination of the colon. Laparoscopy is exploratory procedure of the abdominal cavity using a small scope. Proctosigmoidoscopy is a procedure to examine the sigmoid colon and rectum with a small scope.

103. A. tissue or organ protruding through a cavity or the abdominal wall

A diverticulum is protrusion in the wall of the colon. Varices are varicose veins. A gastrostomy is an artificial opening between the stomach and the abdominal wall.

104. D. all of the above

An aphthous ulceration (canker sore, aphthous ulcer, or aphthous stomatitis) is a painful sore on the mouth or lips caused by the herpes simplex virus.

105. B. pyloric stenosis

Scleroderma does not occur in infants, is atrophy of the lower esophagus smooth muscles, and causes dysphagia esophageal reflex, and strictures. A hiatal hernia occurs in adulthood, which is a condition where the diaphragm goes over the stomach and causes heartburn, belching, reflux, and chest discomfort. Gastritis is an adult condition that results in inflammation of the stomach mucosa and it causes nausea, vomiting, bleeding, pain, and anorexia.

106. C. diverticulitis

Cirrhosis is severe liver damage caused by use and liver damage from drugs or viruses, and symptoms are nausea, vomiting, fatigue, jaundice, and edema. Appendicitis is inflammation of the vermiform appendix that projects from the lumen due to infection, and it causes abdominal pain and fever. Pancreatitis is inflammation of the pancreas caused by alcohol, biliary tract obstruction, drug use, gallstones, and viral infections. It produces abdominal pain, fever, septicemia, and general sepsis. Diverticulitis is inflammation of the diverticula in the colon, an aging condition caused by infection with symptoms of diarrhea, gas, and abdominal pain.

107. C. lymph node

Lymph sends leaked interstitial fluid into the venous system, assists in immune function, and helps with filtering blood. Lymph nodes are small structures of concentrated lymph tissue. The spleen is a tiny organ located in the left upper abdomen area that filters blood. The thymus is a tiny organ that secretes thymosin and matures the T cells. Tonsils are small tissue structures in the throat.

108. A. axillary nodes

The jugular nodes are located in the neck region, the submental nodes are on the jaw region, and the inguinal nodes are near the groin.

109. B. iron deficiency anemia

Aplastic anemia is a group of anemias where bone marrow failure occurs caused by genetics, chemical agents, irradiation, and immunologic factors. Sickle cell anemia involves abnormal sickle-shaped erythrocytes caused by an abnormal type of hemoglobin. Hemolytic anemia is short survival of mature erythrocytes caused by excessive destruction of RBCs.

110. D. acute lymphocytic leukemia (ALL)

CML is slow, progressive disease that occurs more often in those over fifty-five caused by mature and immature granulocytes in the bone marrow and blood. CLL is slowly progressive cancer seen more often in older adults caused by increased numbers of mature lymphocytes. AML is cancer of the blood that has a rapid onset and short survival time that causes fatigue, lymphadenopathy, and bone pain. ALL is cancer of the blood that occurs more often in children and adolescents caused by immature lymphocytes.

111. D. manage various body functions by use of hormones

The endocrine system is composed of various glands, as well as ductless endocrine glands that secrete hormones into the blood. This system manages the body by use of chemical messengers called hormones. Other components of this system are pineal gland, hypothalamus, pituitary gland, parathyroid gland, adrenals glands, the pancreas, ovaries, testis, and thymus.

112. C. pituitary gland

The pituitary gland, also called the master gland or hypophysis, is located at the base of the brain near the sella turcica, and it releases numerous hormones. The thyroid gland is located over the trachea, and it secretes thyroxine and triiodothyronine. The parathyroid gland is located on the posterior region of the thyroid gland, and it secretes parathyroid hormone. The adrenal gland is located on top of each kidney, and it secretes corticosteroids (cortisone, aldosterone, and androgens).

113. C. hypothalamus

The thymus is located behind the sternum, and it produces thymosin. The pancreas is located behind the stomach, and it secretes insulin and glycogen. The pineal gland is located between the two brain cerebral hemispheres, and it secretes melatonin and neurotransmitters.

114. C. both A and B

Diabetes mellitus is a chronic endocrine condition caused by a deficiency in insulin production or poor insulin usage. Both Type I and Type II diabetes produce symptoms of polyuria, polydipsia, glycosuria, and weight loss.

115. D. an overactive adrenal cortex or long-term use of steroids

Hyperthyroidism, also called, thyrotoxicosis is excess production of thyroid hormone caused by an autoimmune process. Hypothyroidism, also called Hashimoto's disease is an underactive thyroid gland caused by inadequate amounts of TSH or poor thyroid hormone production.

Addison's disease, also called primary adrenal insufficiency, is the deficiency of adrenocortical hormones caused by tumors, viruses, autoimmune disorders, infection, and tuberculosis. Cushing's syndrome, also called hypercortisolism, is excessive production of adrenocorticotropic hormone (ACTH) caused by overactive adrenal cortex or long-term use of steroids.

116. A. the cranial nerves and the spinal nerves

The nervous system controls, regulates, and communicates with the various structures, organs, and body parts. It is made up of the Central Nervous System (CNS), which is the brain and spinal cord, and the PNS, which involves the cranial and spinal nerves. Neurons are the primary cells of the nervous system. Types include: dendrites (receive nerve signals), cell body (nucleus), axon (carries nerve signals), and mylein sheath (around the axon). The cerebellum and cerebrum are brain structures.

117. B. 5

There are seven cervical, twelve thoracic, five lumbar, five sacrum, and four coccyx vertebrae.

118. D. discectomy

Craniectomy is partial, permanent removal of the skull. Laminectomy is surgical excision of the posterior region of the vertebra (spinal process). Vertebrectomy is removal of a vertebra. Discectomy is removal of a vertebral disc.

119. B. transient ischemic attack (TIA)

TIA is the temporary reduction of blood flow to the brain, causing stroke-like symptoms from cerebrovascular disease. It produces slurred speech, paresthesia of face, and short term mental confusion. Alzheimer's disease is the most common type of dementia, which is thought to be genetic or autoimmune, and the symptoms are chronic and irreversible memory loss, personality changes, confusion, and restlessness. Amyotrophic lateral sclerosis (ALS), also called Lou Gehrig's disease, is a chronic debilitating condition involving deterioration of the motor neurons, which is caused by familial chromosome twenty-one aberration. It produces difficulty walking, talking, and breathing. MG is a chronic, long-standing condition that involves grave muscle weakness, and it is an auto-immune disease that produces muscle weakness and muscle fatigue.

120. C. smell

Olfactory sense receptors are located in the nasal cavity and associated with CN1.

121. C. aqueous humor

The sclera is the white of the eye that extends from the cornea to the optic nerve. The choroid is the middle layer of the eye that contains pigment. The retina is the inner layer of the eye that contains rods and cones. The aqueous humor is fluid in front of the lens, whereas the vitreous humor is fluid behind the lens.

122. D. tympanic membrane

Ossicles are the small inner ear bones, which include the malleus, incus, and stapes. The auricle, also called the pinna, is the structure that allows sound waves to enter the ear.

123. drooping of the upper eyelid

Dacryocystitis is a blocked nasolacrimal duct, blepharitis is eyelid inflammation, and myopia is nearsightedness.

124. D. fenestration

An apicectomy is removal of a portion of the temporal bone. A mastoidectomy is removal of the mastoid bone. Keratoplasty is surgical repair of the cornea. Fenestration is the creation of a small opening in the middle ear.

125. D. all of the above

Macular degeneration is destruction of the fovea centralis that occurs with age. The main symptom is loss of central vision.

126. B. sensorineural hearing loss

Sensorineural hearing loss is loss of hearing due to lesion of the cochlea or neural path caused by a defect in receptors or vestibulocochlear nerve. Conductive hearing loss is loss of hearing due to defect of sound-conducting apparatus caused by wax buildup or scarring of the tympanic membrane.

127. B. a stye

Conjunctivitis, also called *pink eye*, is where there is inflammation of the lining of the eyelid. Cataracts are clouding of the lens due to protein aggregate accumulation caused by congenital, genetic, trauma, and age. Keratitis is corneal inflammation caused by HSV. A hordeolum is a stye on the eyelid caused by bacterial infection of hair follicle.

128. A. diseases, tabular

International Classification of Diseases (ICD) Ninth Revision (9) Clinical Modifications (CM) (ICD-9-CM) codes are used for reporting various diagnoses. Volume 1 is called *Diseases, Tabular*, Volume 2 is called *Diseases, Index*, and Volume 3 is the hospital version. The use of ICD-9-CM allow for tracking of patients and healthcare costs.

129. A. brackets

Brackets are used to enclose synonyms, explanatory phrases, or alternative wording. Parentheses are used to contain nonessential modifiers, and they do not affect code assignment. Colons are used to complete statements with one or more modifiers. A brace precedes a modifying statement.

130. B. E codes

Section Three of ICD-9 is the *Index to External Causes of Injuries and Poisoning* (E Codes), and these codes are used to provide additional information regarding the exact nature of injury or poisoning.

131. C. to further define or give examples of the content

Included notes appear immediately under a three-digit code title, and their purpose is to further define or give examples of the content. Excluded notes indicate that the terms excluded from the code should be used somewhere else. In some cases, however, the codes for the excluded terms should not be used along with the code from which it is excluded. Inclusion terms are a list of terms included under certain four- and five-digit codes. These terms specify the conditions for which that code number is to be used. The terms are either synonyms of the code title, or other specified code terms indicating various conditions assigned to that code.

132. D. American Medical Association (AMA)

The ICD-9-CM official guidelines were developed by four cooperating parties: American Health Information Management Association (AHIMA), AHA, CMS, and National Center for Health Statistics (NCHS).

133. C. No diagnosis is established or confirmed by a physician.

Codes that describe the signs and symptoms rather than a diagnosis are only used when no diagnosis is established or confirmed by a physician. For someone who may not currently be sick or who receives limited services, the details or circumstances should be recorded as the main condition.

134. A. as long as the patient is receiving care for that diagnosis

Chronic codes are used over and over again, as long as the patient is receiving care for that diagnosis.

135. B. Assign the V code first, followed by a secondary code describing the reason for the non-routine test.

For routine laboratory/radiology testing in the absence of signs, symptoms, or associated diagnosis, assign V72.5 and/or a code from subcategory V72.6. If routine testing is performed during the same encounter to evaluate a sign, symptom, or diagnosis, assign the V code first, followed by a secondary code describing the reason for the non-routine test.

136. C. Use an appropriate V code first, followed by a secondary code for the diagnosis or problem that requires treatment.

For a patient who is receiving chemotherapy, radiation therapy, or rehabilitation, use an appropriate V code first, followed by a secondary code for the diagnosis or problem that requires treatment.

137. B. Use a code that incorporates multiple conditions as the *main* code.

When an episode of healthcare involves a number of related conditions, the one that is clearly more severe and demands the most resources should be recorded as the first-listed diagnosis. Where no one condition predominates, use a code that incorporate multiple conditions as the *main* code.

138. D. V65.44 HIV counseling

For patients receiving HIV screening results, use code V65.44 HIV counseling. Code for HIV and HIV-related illness only if it is listed as a confirmed diagnosis: 042 HIV vs. 795.71 Nonspecific HIV serology. Never assign code 042 HIV for asymptomatic disease or nonspecific blood work. For HIV screening, use code V73.89 Screening for other specified viral disease.

139. A. Go to the Neoplasm Table in the Alphabetic Index.

To code for neoplasms, first locate the histologic type (sarcoma, melanoma, etc.), which is found in the Neoplasm Table in Index under *N*. Then find the code by body site. The Neoplasm Table is divided into columns: Malignant, Benign, Uncertain behavior, and Unspecified.

140. A. First code for the treatment, followed by a secondary neoplasm code.

The first-listed code will be a V code for the treatment, followed by a secondary code for the neoplasm.

141. B. the fracture

If a pathological fracture occurs due to the neoplasm, the sequencing is related to the focus of treatment. For instance, an encounter focused on treating the fracture will be coded first, followed by the code for the primary neoplasm.

142. C. malignant neoplasm, unspecified

When there is extensive metastasis, the coder should assign the code for Disseminated malignant neoplasm, unspecified. The code used when the physician is unable to determine the site of primary malignancy is Malignant neoplasm, unspecified.

143. D. a code for Type II diabetes mellitus, followed by a secondary code for Long-term use of insulin.

When it is documented that the patient uses insulin, but the type of diabetes is not recorded, the coder should use a code for Type II diabetes mellitus, followed by a secondary code for Long-term use of insulin.

144. B. type II diabetes

If the type of diabetes mellitus is not documented in the medical record the default diagnosis is Type II diabetes.

145. B. Use code 996.57, Mechanical complication due to insulin pump, as the principal code for an encounter due to an insulin pump malfunction resulting in an overdose of insulin, followed by code 962.3, Poisoning by insulin.

An underdose of insulin due to insulin pump failure should first be assigned code 996.57, Mechanical complication due to insulin pump, followed by the appropriate diabetes mellitus code. Use code 996.57, Mechanical complication due to insulin pump, as the principal code for an encounter due to an insulin pump malfunction resulting in an overdose of insulin, followed by code 962.3, poisoning by insulin.

146. B. Use first a code to identify the substance, followed by the anemia code.

For aplastic anemia that is drug-induced or due to other external causes, a code should be used first to identify the substance, followed by the anemia code.

147. C. not the primary reason for the encounter, but is included in the visit

Subcategory 285.2, Anemia in chronic illness, has codes for anemia in chronic kidney disease, code 285.21; anemia in neoplastic disease, code 285.22; and anemia in other chronic illness, code 285.29. If the encounter is for treatment of the anemia, these codes can be used as the principal diagnosis code. They may also be used as secondary codes if treatment of the anemia is not the primary reason for the encounter, but is included in the visit. Also, a secondary code for the chronic condition causing the anemia should be listed.

148. D. 3 – chronic

Codes in chapter five include personality disorders, neuroses, psychoses, stress disorders, and sexual deviation conditions. The fifth digit represents the status of the episode: 0 (unspecified), 1 (continuous), 2 (episodic), and 3 (in remission).

149. D. First code for the underlying condition, followed by a secondary code for Delirium due to known physiological condition.

If delirium is due to a known physiological condition, the coder should code first the underlying condition, followed by a code for Delirium due to known physiological condition.

150. A. The provider has specifically documented this as a diagnosis.

Avoid the use of the code for Central pain syndrome and Chronic pain syndrome unless the provider has specifically documented this as a diagnosis.

151. D. all of the above

If the pain is not specified as acute or chronic, avoid use of codes from category 338, except for post-thoracotomy pain, postoperative pain, neoplasm related pain, or central pain syndrome.

152. C. code 338.3

Code 338.3 is assigned to pain documented as being related, associated with, or due to cancer, a tumor, or a primary or secondary malignancy. This code is assigned regardless of whether the pain is acute or chronic. Codes from Pain subcategories 338.1 and 338.2 are used for pain control and should not be listed first if the underlying (definitive) diagnosis is known. Acute pain is classified to subcategory 338.1, and chronic pain is classified to subcategory 338.2.

153. B. the Alphabetic List under *H*

There are three types of hypertension: Malignant (accelerated, poor prognosis, severe), Benign (continuous, mild, controllable), and Unspecified (not otherwise indicated). To classify hypertension, the coder must use the hypertension table, which is located in the Alphabetic Index of ICD-9-CM under *H*.

154. C. Code from the subcategory 403 and assign a fifth digit of 0.

In subcategory 403, hypertensive chronic kidney disease, assign a fifth digit for the stage of disease (0-CKD stage one through four and 1-CKD stage five or end stage).

155. D. with a code for TIA, followed by code for cerebral infarction without residual deficits

For history of cerebrovascular accident (CVA) with no neurologic deficits, assign code V12.54, TIA, followed by a code for the cerebral infarction without residual deficits.

156. C. first-listed code for peritonsillar abscess, followed by a secondary code for the infectious agent

The coder must use an additional code for the infectious agent when reporting peritonsillar abscess as the first-listed code.

157. A. first assign a code for the lung condition, followed by a secondary code for Personal history of nicotine dependence

When coding a chronic condition for a patient who has a history of smoking, the coder would first assign a code for the lung condition, followed by a secondary code for Personal history of nicotine dependence.

158. A. Explain to the patient that the HIV must be reported, and code the HIV disease first, followed by the code for the respiratory condition.

If a patient is admitted with a respiratory condition related to HIV, the HIV disease must be reported prior to the code for the respiratory condition.

159. C. Code first for the gingivitis, followed by a secondary code for History of tobacco use or Tobacco use.

When coding for periodontal disease, stomatitis, gingivitis, lip disease, tongue disorders, and conditions of the oral mucosa, additional codes should be used to report documented exposure to tobacco smoke, a history of tobacco use, occupational and environmental smoke exposure, tobacco use, or tobacco dependence.

160. B. The first-listed code would be Neuromuscular dysfunction of bladder, followed by a secondary code for Stress incontinence.

For a patient with a neurogenic bladder with stress incontinence, the first-listed code would be Neuromuscular dysfunction of bladder, followed by a secondary code for Stress incontinence.

161. A. 0 – Unknown

Chapter eleven has extensive multiple coding requirements and use of a fifth digit. For many codes, a fifth digit denotes current episode of care (0-Unspecified, 1-Delivered, with or without antepartum condition, 2-Delivered, with mention of postpartum complication, 3-Antepartum condition/complication, and 4-Postpartum condition/complication).

162. D. Code first for the illness or injury, followed by the secondary code V22.2, Pregnant state incidental.

When a pregnant woman has an injury or illness, the code for the injury or illness is listed first, followed by the secondary code V22.2 Pregnant state incidental.

163. B. 1

Abortion codes require a fifth digit (0-Unspecified, 1-Incomplete, and 2-Complete).

164. B. with code 648.0x, Diabetes mellitus complicating pregnancy, followed by a secondary code from category 250, Diabetes mellitus

Pregnant women who are diabetic should be assigned code 648.0x, Diabetes mellitus complicating pregnancy. To identify the type of diabetes, use a secondary code from category 250, Diabetes mellitus, or category 249, Secondary diabetes.

165. C. First list a code for the ultraviolet radiation, followed by a code for the type of skin condition.

For coding skin changes from exposure to radiation, the source of ultraviolet radiation should be first reported with an additional code for the type of skin condition.

166. B. with a first-listed code for Foreign body of the soft muscle tissue, followed by a secondary code for the type of foreign body

If a patient has infective myositis, interstitial myositis, or a foreign body of the soft muscle tissue, a secondary code is needed to identify the infectious agent or foreign body.

167. A. with a first-listed code for Liveborn, followed by secondary codes for Low birth weight and immaturity status and a code to document the anomaly

The main diagnosis on the birth record for a newborn should be assigned a code for Liveborn, according to place of birth and type of delivery. If a newborn, child, or adult patient has a history of being born prematurely or having low birth weight that affects the current status of health, the coder should use a secondary code for Low birth weight and immaturity status. If a child is born with a congenital anomaly, the first-listed code should be Liveborn infant, followed by a code to document the anomaly.

168. C. First list a code to identify the drug, followed by a secondary code for urinary retention.

When urinary retention is due to a medication, the coder should first list a code to specify the drug, followed by a code for the urinary retention

169. D. First list a code for the first-degree burn, followed by secondary codes for the second-degree burns.

When coding for burns, sequence the highest degree burn first, followed by secondary codes for other degree burns.

170. A. Code first with the poisoning code, followed by a secondary code for the overdose and an additional code for drug abuse or dependence to the substance.

For poisoning or a reaction due to improper medication use, code first with the poisoning code, followed by a secondary code for the manifestation. Also, use an additional code if there is also a diagnosis of drug abuse or dependence to the substance.

171. D. newborn prematurity status

The four circumstances include those listed by choices A, B, C, as well as newborn birth status.

172. D. all of the above

Status codes from chapter 18 of ICD-9-CM indicate that a patient is a carrier of a disease, has the sequelae or residual of a past condition, or has another factor influencing health status. This includes such things as the presence of prosthetic or mechanical devices resulting from past treatment.

173. B. when it is documented by the provider

Code V49.86, Do not resuscitate status, may be used when it is documented by the provider that a *do not resuscitate* status exists.

174. A. V56.6x, Long-term (current) drug use

Code V58.6x, Long-term (current) drug use, indicates a patient's continuous use of a prescribed drug for the long-term therapy of a condition or for preventive use, not for an addiction to a substance.

175. D. that a patient has a high risk for contracting a disease, disorder, or condition because a patient has a family member(s) who has or had a particular disease

Family history codes are used to show that a patient has a high risk for contracting a disease, disorder, or condition because a patient has a family member(s) has or had a particular disease.

176. A. never the first-listed diagnosis

An E code is never the first-listed diagnosis. E codes are used with any code in the range of 001 - V91, which indicates an injury, poisoning, or adverse effect due to an external cause. An activity E code may be used with any code in the range of 001 - V91 that indicates an injury, health condition due to an activity, or the activity that contributed to a condition. Assign the E code for the initial encounter of an injury, poisoning, or adverse effect of drugs, but never for subsequent treatment. External cause of injury codes may also be assigned along with acute fracture codes.

177. D. Z codes

Z codes represent factors that influence health status and contact with health services, which are recorded as diagnoses. The V, W, X, and Y codes are used to indicate the external causes of injuries and conditions.

178. D. a first-listed code for the fracture, followed by a secondary code for the terrorism event and a tertiary code for the bus accident

If two or more events cause separate injuries, assign an E code for each cause. The first-listed E code is selected in the following order: (1) E codes for child and adult abuse, (2) E codes for terrorism events, (3) E codes for cataclysmic events, and (4) E codes for transport accidents. Never list E codes first.

179. C. the fifth character dummy placeholder for many 6-character codes

With ICD-10-CM, the letter *x* is used as the fifth character dummy placeholder for many six-character codes, as in T37.5x1 (poisoning by antiviral drugs, accidental). This is done to allow for expansion in the future, where the sixth character has a specific use. For example, the T36 – T50 codes represent poisoning or adverse effects and the T51 – T65 codes represent toxic effects. The sixth character in these categories represents the indent: accidental, assault, intentional self-harm, undetermined, underdosing, or adverse effect.

180. D. all of the above

ICD-10-CM codes have three- to seven-digit alphanumeric codes; describe diseases, illnesses, injuries, procedures, and signs/symptoms; and have one or more definitions.

181. A. strategic planning and healthcare delivery system design

The ICD-10-CM classification system offers many benefits. This coding measure will allow for improved measurement of safety, quality, and efficacy of care, designed payment systems and claims processing for reimbursement, conduction of research, clinical trials, and epidemiological studies, health policy, strategic planning and healthcare delivery system design, financial, clinical, and administrative performance, ability to track public health and risks for diseases, prevention and detection of healthcare fraud and abuse, and monitoring of resource utilization.

182. B. both systems use *unspecified* and *not otherwise specified* codes when a more specific code is not available

Both systems use a Tabular List and Alphabetic Index. Both Tabular lists are structured similarly, except with the ICD-10-CM, the Sense Organs are separated from the Nervous System chapter. In both systems, codes are invalid if they are missing an applicable character. Codes are looked up the same way in both systems, with diagnostic terms from the Alphabetic Index and verified code number from the Tabular List. Both systems use *unspecified* and *not otherwise specified* codes when a more specific code is not available.

183. A. In the ICD-9-CM, codes are invalid if they are missing an applicable character, whereas in the ICD-10-CM they would be valid.

In both systems, codes are invalid if they are missing an applicable character. Additionally, ICD-10-CM codes are more specific than ICD-9-CM codes. ICD-10-CM codes have letter and numbers (alphanumeric), with the first character a letter. ICD-10-CM codes are longer than ICD-9-CM codes, with up to seven characters. ICD-10-CM codes are more complete, so the coder does not need to refer back to the category or subcategory level.

184. D. cross-reference notes

Cross-reference notes are found in the Alphabetic Index and include *see, see also, see category*, and *see condition*. They advise the coder to look somewhere else before assigning a code.

185. C. due to

Relational terms of ICD-10-CM include *and, with*, and *due to*. *And* means both *and* and *or* when it is found in the code title. The word *with* means *associated with* or *due to* when it is found in the code title and as an instructional note in the Tabular List. In the Alphabetic Index, the word *with* is sequenced immediately following the main term. The words *due to*, in both the Tabular List and the Alphabetic Index, mean that there is a casual relationship between two conditions. This assumption occurs when both conditions are present or when the diagnostic statement indicates this relationship.

186. C. Healthcare Common Procedure Coding System

There are two levels of HCPCS codes: Level I codes, which are alphaneumeric CPT codes and Level II codes, which are known as National Codes. Healthcare Common Procedure Coding System (HCPCS) was established in 1978 to standardize the reporting of various medical procedures, products, supplies, and services.

187. D. holter monitors

The HPCSC codes cover nonphysician services, but not diagnostic testing.

188. C. C

Code category A is used for Transportation, Medical/Surgical Supplies, Experimental, and Miscellaneous. Code category B is used for Enteral and Parenteral Therapy. Code category C is used for Temporary Hospital Outpatient Prospective Payment System. Code category G is used for Temporary Procedures and Professional Services.

189. B. –E1

Modifier –LT is used for left side, but –E1 is used for upper left, eyelid. Modifier –F1 is used for left hand, second digit.

190. D. none of the above

Medicare is an insurance program established in 1966 for those sixty-five years of age and older. The persons covered are called *beneficiaries*. This system also covers disabled persons.

191. D. part D

The basic structure of the Medicare program is Part A, which includes hospital and institutional care coverage, Part B, which includes Supplemental and Nonhospital Care Coverage, Part C, which includes Medicare Advantage Organization (MAO) Plans, and Part D, the Prescription Drug Plan (PDP), which includes Medicare Advantage Plans (MA-PDs), private prescription drug plans (PDPs), and premiums paid by the beneficiary.

192. A. to promote national coding methods and control improper coding and reimbursement

The National Correct Coding Initiative (NCCI) was developed by CMS to promote national coding methods and control improper coding and reimbursement. This includes *unbundling*, which is billing multiple procedure codes for services covered by a single comprehensive code. Quality improvement organizations (QIOs) were established by CMS to ensure quality of patient care, see that Medicare only pays for necessary and reasonable services, and protect the beneficiaries.

193. B. the Resource-Based Relative Value Scale (RBRVS)

The RBRVS is a form of physician payment reform implemented in 1992. This established the National Fee Schedule (NFS), which is a RBRVS payment method that allows payment of eighty percent. It is used by both suppliers and physicians. Relative Value Units (RVUs) are national unit values assigned to each Current Procedure Terminology (CPT) code. These involve malpractice costs, overhead costs, and the work and skilled required for the procedure.

194. C. the AMA

The AMA provides healthcare professionals with information related to public policy and insurance concerns. CPT codes are a set of codes that describe numerous medical and surgical procedures and services. They are used to report surgical procedures, medical treatments, diagnostic testing, and provider services in outpatient and inpatient settings.

195. B. category II codes

Category I CPT codes are five-digit numeric codes used to report procedures that are consistent with contemporary medical practice. These codes are used by healthcare providers when reporting procedures and services. Category II CPT codes are supplemental tracking codes used for performance evaluation. For compliance with HIPAA regulations, the codes facilitate the collection of data regarding quality of care. They are alphanumeric codes, with four digits numbers followed by the alpha character *F*. Category III are temporary codes for new and emerging technologies. There are no Category IV codes.

196. D. all of the above

Level I CPT and HCPCS codes contain modifiers, which are two-digit codes that can be numeric, alphanumeric, or alpha. This allows for more specific reporting. Modifier functions include altered, bilateral, multiple, only portions of service, and more than one surgeon.

197. B. -23

Modifier -22: Increased Procedural Service indicates that the services required more time and supplies than usual. Modifier -24: Unrelated E/M Services by Same Physician During a Postoperative Period indicates that the services is not related to the surgery. Modifier -25: Significant, Separately Identifiable E/M Service, by Same Physician on the Same Day of the Procedure, or Other Service indicates that there was more than one service.

198. C. that the same procedure was performed on different sites, that multiple procedures were performed, or that the procedure was performed multiple times

Modifier -26: Professional Component indicates that the physician was involved. Modifier -50: Bilateral Procedure indicates that a procedure was performed on organs that are bilateral, such as kidneys or lungs. Modifier -53: Discontinued Procedure indicates that the procedure was started but then stopped for some reason.

199. D. -99

Modifier -90: Reference Laboratory is used when the physician has a business relationship with an outside laboratory. Modifier -91: Repeat Clinical Diagnostic Laboratory Test is used when a laboratory test must be repeated on the same day. Modifier -92: Alternative Laboratory Platform Testing is used to report a laboratory test performed by a portable instrument.

200. D. observation patient

The patient status is either: (1) new patient, (2) established patient, (3) outpatient, or (4) inpatient.

201. all of the above

Level of E/M service is based on those items listed in A, B, and C, as well as key components (history, physical examination, and medical decision making) and contributing factors (coordination of care, presenting problem, and counseling).

202. B. the patient status

The three elements are the problem, data, and the level of risk.

203. C. moderate-complexity

With straightforward MDM, the number of diagnoses and management options is minimal, the risk of complications or death is minimal, and the amount of complexity is either none or minimal. With low-complexity MDM, the number of diagnoses and management options limited, the amount of complexity of data is also limited, and the risk of death or complications is low. With moderate-complexity MDM, the number of diagnoses and management options is multiple, the risk of death or complications is moderate, and the amount of complexity is also moderate. With high-complexity MDM, the number of diagnoses and management options is extensive, the amount of complexity of data is also extensive, and the risk of death or complication is high.

204. D. Hospital Inpatient Services (99221-99239)

New Patient (99201-99205) codes are used for all new patients seen by the physician. Established Patient (99211-99215) codes are used for all returning patients and do not require a physician's presence. Hospital Observation Status (99217-99236) codes are used for patients not ill enough to be admitted, but those that require monitoring. Initial Observation Care (99218-99220) codes are used for the first day if the overnight stay is less than 48 hours. Hospital Inpatient Services (99221-99239) are used for patients admitted to the hospital setting. Consultation Services (99241-99255) codes are used for physician consultations in outpatient and inpatient settings.

205. C. both A and B

Care Plan Oversight Services (99374-99380) are used to report physician supervision of patient care in the home health agency or hospice setting.

206. D. endobronchial

General anesthesia is given to render the patient unconscious. Endotracheal is general anesthesia given through the mouth. Regional anesthesia is a nerve block that does not result in unconsciousness Epidural is regional anesthesia given by injection into the epidural space. Local anesthesia is given to one area by injection or topical application.

207. B. (B + T + M) x Conversion Factor

B = Base Units, which are national unit values for anesthesia services. T = Time, which is the amount of time required for the service. M = Modifying Unit, which is additional units based on the physical status of the patient.

208. C. 7

The subsections include: Diagnostic Radiology, Diagnostic Ultrasound, Radiologic Guidance, Breast Mammography, Bone and Joint Studies, Radiation Oncology, and Nuclear Medicine.

209. A. traditional component (TC)

The Professional Component is the physician portion of service for supervision of technician, interpretation of results, and written report. Modifier -26 is used for this. The Technical Component (TC) is the technician or technologist services, as well as equipment, film, and supplies. Modifier -TC is used for this. The Global Component includes both professional and technical portions.

210. D. Nuclear Medicine (78000 - 79999)

Diagnostic Radiology (70010 - 76499) codes are used for most standard radiographic procedures, including x-ray, computerized axial tomography (CT scan), magnetic resonance imaging (MRI), and angiography. Diagnostic Ultrasound (76506 - 76999) codes are used for high-frequency sound wave tests, such as amplitude (A-Mode), motion (M-Mode), brightness (B-Scan), and Real-Time (RT-Scan). Radiologic Guidance (77001 - 77032) codes are used for guidance during MRI, CT, fluoroscopes, and other tests. Breast Mammography (77051 - 77084) codes are used for various unilateral and bilateral mammography tests. Radiation Oncology (77261 - 77799) codes are used for various therapeutic radiation procedures, clinical treatment planning, simulation, dosimetry, and clinical brachytherapy. Nuclear Medicine (78000 - 79999) codes are used for various placement of radioactive material into the body, as well as measurement of emissions (Buck, 2013).

211. C. Chemistry (82000 - 84999)

Evocative and Suppression Testing (80400 - 80440) codes are used for measurement of stimulating and suppressing agents. Molecular Pathology (81200 - 81406) codes are used for procedures that report molecular assay. Hematology and Coagulation (85002 - 85999) codes are used for laboratory tests on blood and blood collection.

212. A. collection, processing, and typing of blood

Cytogenetic Studies (88230 - 88299) codes are used for genetic testing on cells and chromosomes. Surgical Pathology (88300 - 88399) codes are used for specimen testing on tissue samples (biopsies). Microbiology (87001 - 87999) codes are used for various microscopic tests to identify organisms. Anatomic Pathology (88000 - 88099) codes are used for autopsies.

213. B. toxoid

Bacteria that cause illness are made nontoxic, and these immunizations are called toxoid. Viruses that cause disease are made inactive, and these are considered vaccines. Passive immunizations will not cause an immune response, and these contain antibodies against various diseases.

214. C. both A and B

Pulmonary (94002 - 94799) codes are used for ventilation diagnostic tests and management therapy.

215. A. hemodialysis

Dialysis (90935 - 90999) codes are used for hemodialysis, ESRD physician services, and miscellaneous dialysis procedures.

216. D. none of the above

Ophthalmology E/M eye codes are used for bilateral eye services.

217. D. neither A nor B

Allergy and Clinical Immunology (95004 - 95199) codes are used for allergy testing and allergen immunotherapy.

218. D. all of the above

Biopsy (11100-11101) codes are used for excision of a small piece of skin, subcutaneous tissue, or mucous membrane tissue. Do not use modifier -51 with a biopsy.

219. C. lancing

Incision and Drainage (100400-10180) codes are used for abscess, cyst, carbuncle, boil, infection, hematoma, and pilonidal cyst. I&D codes involve lancing (cutting into the skin), aspiration (removal of fluid), and gauze or tube insertion (to collect drainage).

220. D. all of the above

Benign/Malignant Lesions (11400-11646) codes are used for removal of lesions including local anesthesia and simple closure. Codes include use of anesthesia and simple closure. Each excised lesion should be reported separately. Layered, intermediate, or complex procedures are reported separately.

221. A. percutaneous

Treatment of a fracture depends on the type and severity of the break. Open repair is done when the surgeon must open the site to reduce or fix the fracture. Closed repair is done when the orthopedic specialist does not have to open the site. Percutaneous repair occurs by insertion of devices through the skin or other site.

222. C. Introduction or Removal (20500-20689)

Wound Exploration (20100-20103) codes include enlargement, removal of foreign body, ligation, debridement, and tissue/muscle repair. Excision (20150-20251) codes are used for bone and muscle biopsies. External Fixation (20690-20697) codes are used for placement of a device that holds the bone in position. Introduction or Removal (20500-20689) are used for aspirations, injections, insertions, removals, applications, and adjustments, as well as for various therapeutic sinus tract injections, catheter placement, and antibiotics injections. For arthrocentesis, report both aspiration and injection with one code, and codes are based on joint size (small, intermediate, and major).

223. A. when the application of a cast or strap is included in the surgical procedure

Casting and Strapping (20939-29799) codes are used for cast applications and use of elastic bandages. Used for initial sprain or fracture treatment for the first cast or strap. Subsequent cast/strap applications are coded separately. The application of a cast or strap is not coded when included in the surgical procedures.

224. D. all of the above

The respiratory system subsection codes are divided by site and procedures (incision or excision).

225. A. always

Diagnostic endoscopy is always included in the surgical endoscopy code.

226. B. bronchial tube = full extent

Always code the full extent of the endoscopy procedure. Example: If the procedure begins at the mouth and ends at the bronchial tube, code for *bronchial tube = full extent*.

227. B. -50

Nose (30000-30999) codes are used for incisions, excisions, introduction, repair, destruction, packing, cauterization, and ligation. Code with modifier -50 when both sides are involved.

228. B. electrocardiogram

Codes in the CPT Cardiovascular System subsection refer to various procedures and services of the heart and vessels. An invasive procedure is when a catheter or surgical instrument must enter the body, such as an incision or percutaneous method. Noninvasive procedures do not rupture the skin, such as electrocardiogram or Doppler studies.

229. D. All of the above

Cardiography (93000 - 93278) codes are used for stress tests, Holter monitors, and electrocardiograms.

230. C. Venous and Arterial Grafting (33517 - 33536)

Heart and Pericardium (33010 - 33999) codes include placing of pacemakers, pacing cardioverter-defibrillators, electrophysiologic operative procedures, patient-activated event recorder placement, and valvular repair. Arteries and Veins (34001 - 37799) codes are used only for noncoronary vessel surgeries, embolectomies, thrombectomies, venous reconstruction, endovascular repair of AAA, and noncoronary bypass grafts. Endovascular Repair of Descending Aorta (33830 - 33891) are used for placement of an endovascular aortic prosthesis or stent-graft procedure. Venous and Arterial Grafting (33517 - 33536) are used for various arterial and venous grafting procedures.

231. A. be bundled

Lymph Nodes and Lymphatic Channels (38300 - 38999) codes are used for lymphadenectomies, which are divided as either limited or radical. A limited lymphadnectomy involves use of pelvic and para-aortic lymph nodes for neoplasm staging. A radical lymphadnectomy involves removal of aortic and splenic lymph nodes, as well as the surrounding tissue. When this procedure is done along with a major procedure, it should be bundled.

232. D. all of the above

General (38204 - 38242) codes are used for bone marrow preservation, preparation, purification, aspiration, biopsy, harvesting, and transplantation, as well as procedures involving stem cells.

233. B. esophagogastroscopy

Esophagoscopy is for esophagus only. Esophagogastroduodenoscopy is for esophagus and past the pyloric channel. Proctosignmoidoscopy is for rectum and the sigmoid colon only. Signmoidoscopy is for rectum, sigmoid colon, and part of the descending colon.

234. D. all of the above

Hernia (49491 - 49659) codes are used for various hernia repairs and surgical procedures related to hernias. These codes are divided by type of hernia (inguinal, umbilical, or femoral), as well as the age of patient, initial or subsequent repair, and clinical presentation (strangulated or incarcerated).

235. C. both A and B

Kidney (50010 - 50593) codes are used endoscopy, stoma, and incision. These codes are used for procedures that are performed through a previously established stoma or incision. The codes can be unilateral or bilateral. Renal catheters can be internally dwelling, externally accessible, for drainage and injection, and for radiography.

236. B. Vesical Neck and Prostate (52400-52700)

Ureter (50600 - 50980) codes are used for incision, excision, introduction, repair, laparoscopy, and endoscopy. These codes can be unilateral or bilateral and are divided by procedure. Bladder (51020 - 52700) codes are used for incision, removal, excision, introduction, urodynamics, repair, and various scopes and procedures. This section includes many bundled codes, so coder must read descriptions with care. Vesical Neck and Prostate (52400-52700) codes are used for TURP procedures.

237. A. cesarean section

Maternity Care and Delivery (59000 - 59899) are used for antepartum care, fetal non-stress tests, fetal monitoring, delivery, Cesarean section, and abortion. Female Genital System (56405 - 58770) codes are used for biopsies, incision, marsupialization, destruction, excision, vulvectomies, conization, endoscopy, laparoscopy, manipulation, and repair.

238. A. extent of procedure

These codes are divided by extent of the procedure (simple or extensive) and method of destruction (cryosurgery, chemical, etc.). Circumcision is included in the excision subheading. Introduction procedures for the corpora cavernosa involve injections and erectile dysfunction treatment.

239. D. neither A nor B

Female Genital System (56405 - 58770) codes are used for biopsies, incision, marsupialization, destruction, excision, vulvectomies, conization, endoscopy, laparoscopy, manipulation, and repair. Destruction codes are divided by complexity of service and method of destruction. Excision codes include anesthetic, biopsy, and simple closure.

240. A. Endocrine System (60000 - 60699)

Nervous System ((61000 - 64999) codes are used for various procedures of the skull, meninges, and brain, base of the skull, and cerebrospinal fluid shunt placement. Eye and Adnexa (65091 - 68899) codes are used for insertion of ocular implants, cataract surgeries, and blepharoplasty. Auditory System (69000 - 69979) codes are used for various procedures of the inner and outer ear, including Eustachian tube placement and removal, myringotomy, and tympanostomy.

Made in the USA
San Bernardino, CA
13 April 2016